May–

Day by Day with God

Rooting women's lives in the Bible

BRF
Ministries

Ministries

15 The Chambers, Vineyard
Abingdon OX14 3FE
+44 (0)1865 319700 | brf.org.uk

Bible Reading Fellowship is a charity (233280)
and company limited by guarantee (301324),
registered in England and Wales

ISBN 978 1 80039 255 7
All rights reserved

Distributed in Australia by:
MediaCom Education Inc, PO Box 610, Unley, SA 5061
Tel: 1 800 811 311 | admin@mediacom.org.au

Distributed in New Zealand by:
Scripture Union Wholesale, PO Box 760, Wellington
Tel: 04 385 0421 | suwholesale@clear.net.nz

Acknowledgements
Scripture quotations marked with the following abbreviations are taken from the version
shown. Where no abbreviation is given, the quotation is taken from the same version as
the headline reference. NIV: The Holy Bible, New International Version (Anglicised edition)
copyright © 1979, 1984, 2011 by Biblica. Used by permission of Hodder & Stoughton
Publishers, a Hachette UK company. All rights reserved. 'NIV' is a registered trademark
of Biblica. UK trademark number 1448790. NLT: The Holy Bible, New Living Translation,
copyright © 1996, 2004, 2007, 2013. Used by permission of Tyndale House Publishers, Inc.,
Carol Stream, Illinois 60188. All rights reserved. TLB: The Living Bible copyright © 1971 by
Tyndale House Foundation. Used by permission of Tyndale House Publishers Inc., Carol
Stream, Illinois 60188. All rights reserved. MSG: *The Message*, copyright © 1993, 1994, 1995,
1996, 2000, 2001, 2002 by Eugene H. Peterson. Used by permission of NavPress. All rights
reserved. Represented by Tyndale House Publishers, Inc. GNT: the Good News Bible published
by The Bible Societies/HarperCollins Publishers Ltd, UK © American Bible Society 1966, 1971,
1976, 1992, used with permission. NRSV: the New Revised Standard Version Updated Edition.
Copyright © 2021 National Council of Churches of Christ in the United States of America. Used
by permission. All rights reserved worldwide.

Song lyrics quoted on p. 101 © Christian Strover / Jubilate Hymns, copyrightmanager@
jubilatehymns.co.uk, USED BY PERMISSION

A catalogue record for this book is available from the British Library

Printed and bound by Gutenberg Press, Tarxien, Malta

Day by Day with God

Edited by **Jackie Harris**

May–August 2024

Writers in this issue

Alianore Smith is church partnerships manager for International Justice Mission UK, having previously worked for the London Institute for Contemporary Christianity. She is author of *Musings of a Clergy Child* (BRF, 2017).

Helen Williams has worked in music, education, management consultancy and administration. She currently finds herself working mostly alongside her husband, an Anglican bishop, while continuing to work as an accompanist.

Fiona Barnard is a TEFL/ESOL teacher, staff member of Friends International and an honorary chaplain at the University of St Andrews, Scotland. She works with international students, encouraging local Christians to reach out in friendship and evangelism to make disciples.

Selina Stone is lecturer in theology at St Mellitus College, focusing on social justice and ethics. She loves exploring the Bible and faith from the perspective of overlooked and underrepresented groups, including women and minorities.

Tanya Marlow is a lecturer in pastoral theology and a popular speaker and writer. She specialises in *narratio divina* (storytelling in biblical studies) and theologies of disability and suffering. Find her at **tanyamarlow.com**.

Sheila Jacobs is a writer, editor and an award-winning author. She lives in rural north Essex, serves as deacon at an Elim church and is a day chaplain at a retreat centre.

Lakshmi Jeffreys inhabits various roles including wife, mother, friend, dog-walker, vicar and others, within and beyond the church. Having discovered the significance of sabbath, she wants to make more effort simply to 'play' in God's presence, both with others and on her own.

Amy Boucher Pye is a writer, speaker, retreat leader and spiritual director. She's the author of six books, including *Transforming Love: How friendship with Jesus changes us* (Form, 2023) and *Holding Onto Hope* (BRF, 2023). Find her at **amyboucherpye.com**.

Claire Musters is a writer, speaker and host of the *Woman Alive* bookclub. Her books include: *Taking Off the Mask* (Authentic Media, 2017), *Everyday Insight: Disappointment and loss* (CWR, 2020) and *Grace-filled Marriage* (Authentic Media, 2021), written with her husband. Find her at **clairemusters.com**.

Catherine Butcher is a freelance writer and editor, an Anglican reader and a member of General Synod. As communications director for HOPE Together for ten years, she wrote magazines and books to help churches make Jesus known.

Welcome

Thank you for joining us in our Bible studies. It is always a pleasure to introduce these notes and to see how our contributors have developed their theme or what they have discovered in familiar stories or passages.

How are you as we move towards the middle of the year? Are things turning out as you expected or are you in a season of change? Are you feeling strong or a bit wobbly? Excited or wary and worried?

I was thinking about writing this letter on Sunday and a song we sang at church reminded me of how important scripture is in reminding us of God's love and faithfulness. The song – 'My Lighthouse' – speaks of how we can trust in God's promises and in his love for us, and this is the message of many of our studies in this issue.

We begin by focusing on God's promises, as each contributor shares a promise that has been important to them. Then we move on to Peter, a favourite character for many people, whose story is such a wonderful encouragement that God can use us as we are. We end our first month with the second part of our study of Hosea and his revelation of God's redeeming love.

As we move into June, we delve into Jesus' teaching in the sermon on the mount, look closely at the creation story and explore what the Bible says about living simply and how this helps us to regain our focus on what is important. Our summer reading continues with Paul's letter to Titus, written to encourage the young man he had commissioned to build up the church on the island of Crete, and stories of God's refreshing and reviving in our themed study on water and springs. We'll learn too how God not only gives us the gift of friends, but also wants to be friends with us, and discover more of God's patience and mercy through the story of Jonah. Our concluding study looks at how God meets with us, often when we least expect it, through the experiences of both Old and New Testament characters.

As you study the scriptures with us over the next four months, may you find God's word to be a lighthouse – lighting the way, guiding your steps and reassuring you of his love and care.

Jackie Harris, Editor

Precious promises

Jackie Harris writes:

The Bible is filled with promises from God. Some have conditions attached: 'If my people, who are called by my name, will humble themselves and pray and seek my face and turn from their wicked ways, then I will hear from heaven, and I will forgive their sin and will heal their land (2 Chronicles 7:14, NIV). Others are unconditional – the promise to all humankind that God would never send another flood (Genesis 9:8–17) demands nothing from us. It is an enduring promise freely given to everyone.

Many of God's promises were given to individuals. We might think of God's promise to Abraham that he would be the father of a nation (Genesis 12:1–2) or God's promise to Joshua that he would be with him as he succeeded Moses and led God's people into Israel (Joshua 1:9). On other occasions, the promises were given to God's people as a community – promises to forgive them, protect them and restore them.

Some promises were fulfilled immediately, others involved a long wait and still others have yet to be fulfilled. What all God's promises have in common is that they are trustworthy. When God says he will do something, we can be sure that he will keep his word. The author of Hebrews affirms: 'Let us hold unswervingly to the hope we profess, for he who promised is faithful' (Hebrews 10:23, NIV).

The promises in our study are all personally chosen by our contributors, special verses that have often stayed with us over many years. They include promises that God will be with us, that he will act for us and guide us. They assure us of his love, that he sees what is happening around us and that he will not leave us. We hope and pray that these verses will speak into your lives too, and that they will encourage you to seek out more of God's promises and to hold on to the promises that God has given you.

The psalmist declares: 'The Lord is trustworthy in all he promises and faithful in all he does' (Psalm 145:13, NIV). God's promises are precious. Let them sink deep into your heart and minister to you in the days ahead.

Never leave us

'The Lord himself goes before you and will be with you; he will never leave you nor forsake you. Do not be afraid; do not be discouraged.' (v. 8, NIV)

When I'm feeling stressed, anxious or fearful I often speak out God's promises to remind myself of his love and care. Some lines that often come to mind are these from Deuteronomy, that God will never leave me nor forsake me. These are God's words through Moses as God's chosen people enter the promised land.

Moses, because of his sins, was not accompanying God's people into the land of milk and honey. But he was passing along the promises of the God who loved his people and who loved him, who spoke to him face to face, as we'll explore at the end of July. God knew that the Israelites would face challenges and hardships, and he wanted them to hold on to his promise that he'd never abandon them. When times got tough, they could count on him.

Note how God repeats his encouragement that he won't leave or forsake them first to his people (v. 6) and then to Joshua, God's newly appointed leader (v. 8). Both Joshua and the Israelites would face their own specific trials and tests, and God wanted to assure them that they'd never be on their own.

We might feel abandoned by God when we walk through the valley of death and despair. He might appear silent. Even if we can't discern his presence, we can believe that he hasn't left us. We can return to these promises, hanging on as if by our fingernails. And perhaps after the storm has passed, we'll discern that, when we thought we would lose our grip at any moment, God's arms were underneath us the whole time, giving us a firm foundation.

God who leads me through the dark valley, light the path before me so I don't trip and fall. I know that you are next to me and behind me, before me and beside me, because you love me. Amen.

AMY BOUCHER PYE

The battle belongs to the Lord

'Do not be afraid or discouraged because of this vast army. For the battle is not yours, but God's… You will not have to fight this battle. Take up your positions; stand firm and see the deliverance the Lord will give you… Do not be afraid' (vv. 15 and 17, NIV)

Last year, a very difficult situation in our life reached the point where we could no longer continue without something changing. I hope you'll forgive me for not sharing the details, but what I'm privileged to share is how God spoke through this promise, galvanising us, teaching us to trust and to wait for him to act.

The original story is inspiring – Jehoshaphat is under attack but his first thought is to 'enquire of the Lord' (v. 3), to fast and to gather the people to seek the Lord. He leads his people in a wonderful prayer (vv. 6–12) and then 'the Spirit of the Lord came on Jahaziel' (v. 14). These verses contain God's promise to his people – a promise that makes little human sense: the battle you have to fight is 'not yours, but God's' and all you have to do is 'take up your positions; stand firm and see the deliverance the Lord will give you'. Extraordinary!

When we realised the time had come to act, these were the verses that came to me, accompanied by a picture of a domino run set up waiting. God said, 'Just tip the first domino and the rest will follow.' The day we knew this had to happen, a hamper of gifts arrived, completely out of the blue, from someone knowing nothing of our situation. It was the same the next day and the next!

It's never easy to call out something wrong, but this was God's battle. Before long we were taken right away from the action, our only role to take up our position of prayer, to 'stand firm' and to watch and wait. Within months, a significant part of the battle was won and over the rest of the year the final dominos fell.

Chapter 20 ends thus: 'And the kingdom of Jehoshaphat was at peace, for his God had given him rest on every side' (v. 30). Help us not to take battles into our own hands, Lord, but to stand firm and trust you. Amen.

HELEN WILLIAMS

The God who sees

But you, God, see the trouble of the afflicted; you consider their grief and take it in hand. The victims commit themselves to you; you are the helper of the fatherless. (v. 14, NIV)

In my day job – when I'm not writing Bible studies – I work for a large anti-slavery organisation. With an estimated 50 million people trapped in slavery today (International Labour Organization, 2022), it can be easy to feel overwhelmed by the problem and wonder where God is in the midst of it all. Sometimes I feel lost for words when I try to pray for this issue, for all those individuals trapped in unspeakable situations.

The psalms are a great place to turn to when you are at a loss for words to pray. Psalm 10 in particular has been of great encouragement to me over the last few years in my work. It starts with a question: 'Why, Lord, do you stand far off? Why do you hide yourself in times of trouble?' (v. 1) – or, translated into my words: 'God, where did you go? Why are you silent when everything seems awful?'

This psalm takes us on a journey through the reality of evil – those who think they can get away with perpetrating harm because they believe 'God will never notice; he covers his face and he never sees' (v. 11). It puts into words that which we find unspeakable.

But these final verses are the promise and prayer that I cling to – day in, day out – when faced with seemingly impossible situations: God sees. He considers the grief of those who are victims, those who are suffering – and he takes it in hand. He does not forget it. He holds on to it. He sees and he knows. He defends those who are defenceless (v. 18), and he listens to their cry.

The Lord is King forever and ever. Even in the face of suffering and brokenness, of evil and harm. That's a promise I want to stake my hope on.

Father God, thank you that you give us scripture so we have words to pray when we don't know what to say. Thank you that you care for those who seem to be forgotten and listen to their cry. Amen.

ALIANORE SMITH

The shepherd's tender care

He makes me lie down in green pastures, he leads me beside quiet waters, he refreshes my soul. (vv. 2–3a, NIV)

This is such a well-known psalm, but it is full of promises about God's care, and it is the psalm he has drawn me back to in a season of heart-ache and pain. In the midst of 'the darkest valley' – of grief, supporting a family member as they grapple with mental ill-health and navigating the perplexing world of the menopause – I have experienced the shepherd's tender guidance.

He has shown me how to cling to him in the moments of despair, to utilise the treasures that he has prepared and to take time to rest in his presence. I have found new ways to refresh my soul, including the weekly Wednesday worship sessions with Lou and Nathan Fellingham on Facebook.

I am reminded of a friend who had to go into hospital for a procedure. She has tremendous energy and doesn't often slow down, but this particular illness enforced rest. She experienced so much of what is described in this psalm. As she was feeling anxious about going into hospital, a small group of us prayed for her and we felt he was reminding her of Psalm 23 again. She texted from the hospital room to say that she felt at peace, and she knew God was looking out for her as the walls were painted green; she was in her very own 'green pastures'!

When we are in the midst of difficulties, it is so reassuring to sense God's shepherding rod and staff – but he also uses them to lovingly redirect us when we've gone wayward. He provides good things for us to feast on to help us endure too. If life is tough for you right now, ask the good shepherd to open your spiritual eyes to see how he is at work caring for you.

Take time in God's presence today: pull up a chair to the spot he has specially reserved for you. You are so precious, known and loved by him – he hasn't forgotten you and is caring for you.

CLAIRE MUSTERS

God prepares the way

'For I know the plans I have for you,' declares the Lord, 'plans to prosper you and not to harm you, plans to give you hope and a future'. (NIV)

Despite so many warnings, the people of God had lost their land, the temple and their freedom. Now in exile, Jeremiah was telling them their current state would not last forever. Meanwhile, they were to get on with daily life, where they were. In time, God would deliver them. This promise was true then, and it has been my experience, as I feel God has prepared the way at every stage of my life.

Coming to faith from a Hindu background and messing up my A-levels left me with a sense of having disappointed my parents – feeling exiled from them. A teacher at school had led me to Christ and gave me this verse from Jeremiah. Three years later, as an unhappy final year university student, I was introducing new students to a Christian society. One girl mentioned the church where my former teacher had been and then exclaimed, 'You're Lakshmi! The teacher was in my parents' home group. We used to pray for you every week.' I realised my time at university, while not chosen (a significant feature of exile), was still held by God.

I usually become aware of God's plans for me in retrospect. It felt important to support a ministry in my church, rather than pursue a career elsewhere. Four years later, one of the church leaders encouraged me to pursue ordained ministry. Later, as I was discerning where to train, I sensed a call to a particular college. Against the odds, I was offered a place. A year later, in a friend's placement church, I discovered the teacher who brought me to faith!

As I look back, I see how God has fulfilled his promise and enabled me to prosper. Currently I am seeking a new job and trusting again that God will give me hope and a future.

Thank you, loving God, that your plans are not blueprints. You prepare the way; you are faithful in all circumstances and bring unexpected joy. Teach us to look back with the Holy Spirit and to look ahead with hope in Christ. Amen.
LAKSHMI JEFFREYS

A gift for today

The faithful love of the Lord never ends! His mercies never cease. Great is his faithfulness; his mercies begin afresh each morning. (NLT)

I was familiar with these verses long before I actually read the book of Lamentations. It came as a surprise to find them in the midst of such sorrow and lament. Jeremiah writes these words from a place of deep anguish. For years he had been calling God's people to repent and warning that judgement would come, but they had continued to rebel against God and now the city of Jerusalem had been destroyed and her people ruthlessly killed or scattered. Jeremiah is heartbroken by what he has witnessed and yet, even as he remembers the suffering and says he will never get over the loss, he finds hope as he remembers God's love and mercy, which has no end and is given afresh every day.

This is such a wonderful promise not only on those days when we are at our wits' end, when the way ahead seems too difficult or when we feel we've nothing else to give, but also on those days when we wake feeling tired, when we're uninspired by what lies ahead or when we've simply got out on the wrong side of the bed. God's mercy awaits us every day, a fresh batch of God's love and faithfulness available to us each and every morning. Let's ensure we receive that gift today.

My mum often talks about God's loving touches. It might be something as simple as a fine day, a butterfly spreading its wings, an unexpected letter from a friend, a chance meeting or a kind gesture. Such things speak to her of God's love and care for her. What might God's loving touches look like for you? Where did you see God's faithful love and mercy manifesting in your life yesterday? How might you share God's love and mercy with someone else?

Take time to listen to the song 'Great is thy faithfulness' (Thomas Chisholm, 1866–1960) and dwell on the truth that God's mercy is new every morning.

JACKIE HARRIS

Waiting on God

'Write down the revelation and make it plain on tablets so that a herald may run with it. For the revelation awaits an appointed time… Though it linger, wait for it; it will certainly come and will not delay.' (NIV)

This promise from God to act has also been my commission as a writer and editor. I trained as a newspaper journalist because I wanted to learn to write plainly about Jesus in the language that most people find easy to understand. Throughout my career I have worked with visionaries, often helping them by making their vision plain. In recent years that has been helping Roy Crowne share the vision of HOPE Together – challenging churches to work together to make Jesus known with words and action. The churches we worked with were like Habakkuk's heralds who ran with the message.

Like Habakkuk, I have cried out to God about prayers that seem to go unanswered: 'O Lord, how long must I call for help before you will listen?' (1:2, TLB). Like Habakkuk, I see sin and sadness all around me. The law is not enforced. Often there is no justice given in the courts. There are heartless wars. The rich get richer with ill-gotten gains. We see forests cut down, then climate change has a disproportionate impact on the poorest countries.

Like Habakkuk, I long for the time when 'the earth will be filled with the knowledge of the glory of the Lord' (2:14). With my writing, I have sought to hasten that time.

In his dialogue with God, Habakkuk is struggling with the apparent injustice in the world and is questioning why God is allowing the wicked to prosper while the righteous suffer. He is writing to the people and leaders of Judah, in a time of political upheaval, economic instability, moral decay and social injustice – sounds like contemporary Britain!

Habakkuk's message was one of warning and judgement, but also one of hope and faith in God's ultimate justice and redemption. Be patient, Habakkuk says. God's time will come.

Let's pray with Habakkuk for our nation: 'In this time of our deep need, begin again to help us, as you did in years gone by. Show us your power to save us. In your wrath, remember mercy' (3:2, TLB). Amen.

CATHERINE BUTCHER

I am with you

'Go out and train everyone you meet, far and near, in this way of life, marking them by baptism… Instruct them in the practice of all I have commanded you. I'll be with you as you do this, day after day after day, right up to the end of the age.' (MSG)

Yesterday, I set my hair on fire. I was lighting a candle when, in seconds, hot flames were sparking by my left ear. I beat them out and then combed the burnt remains from my hair. Ironically, my intention had been to focus in prayer, reminding myself of God's presence as the candle's light and scent filled the room. What I achieved was panic and a house permeated with the pungent odour of smouldering hair. Once disaster had been averted, the candle was useless because all I could smell was the stench right next to my nose from what remained of my hair. Frightened by what might have happened, I blew it out.

As I pondered my stupidity, I felt a sensuous parable had been dramatically enacted before me. Sometimes in exasperation or bemusement, I ask, 'Where are you, Jesus? I know in my head that you are everywhere, but it doesn't feel like it. Our society cries out for the fragrance of your lovely presence. We so need your light in this darkness!' Trauma or tragedy, wilful or careless mistakes, God-denying attitudes or distractions can so fill our lives and our world that all we experience is burning and danger and fear. The candle of God's felt presence is blown out.

Yet God tells us repeatedly that he is with us. Even in the darkness. In Jesus, God absorbs into himself all the stinking aroma of sin and suffering. For me, some hours later, fresh breeze and some shampoo restored my environment. Cleansed and breathing in his Spirit, our healing still requires time. In the interim, it takes faith to light the candle, to tell a world in crisis that Jesus is close. It requires trust to share his light and sweet aroma as we carry out his mission.

'Because of Christ, we give off a sweet scent rising to God, which is recognised by those on the way of salvation – an aroma redolent with life' (2 Corinthians 2:14–15). How might you spread the fragrance of Jesus today?

FIONA BARNARD

Closeness and fruitfulness

'I am the vine; you are the branches. If you remain in me and I in you, you will bear much fruit; apart from me you can do nothing.' (NIV)

The Bible is filled with images from nature which help us to understand spiritual truths that might be challenging for us. In this passage Jesus is talking to his disciples about the connection they have by drawing on the analogy of a vine. This might not be the most obvious image for us in the UK – unless you have spent a lot of time in a warmer climate – but it would have been perfect for those Jesus was speaking to. He wants them to understand that their lives, their thriving and spiritual health all depend upon their connection to him. Just like a branch needs to be connected to the vine that stores and carries around all the nutrients which keep branches healthy, so the disciples need to be sustained by their oneness with Jesus.

This is a great promise which keeps me connected to God in the middle of a busy life. First, I am reminded that God is aware of what I need. So often we can imagine God to be distant and unaware of what is happening or what is causing us distress, but the image of the vine and 'remain in me and I in you' conveys closeness and unity between God and ourselves. Second, it reminds me that God desires for me to be fruitful, just as I desire that for myself. I have a great awareness of the shortness of life and hopes for what I might get to be and do in my lifetime, and here we see that this is also important to God. This does not mean we should be anxious – fruitfulness is not about being even busier, but about having a life which blesses, feeds and serves others and God, from a place of connection with God. God promises we will not just be fruitful in a small way, but that we will bear much fruit. And a garden full of fruitful vines means that all who are hungry will be fed.

Imagine yourself as a branch on the vine, who is Christ. Do you feel dry or nourished? Are you being fruitful in the way you hope or are you disappointed by the harvest? Bring these thoughts to God in prayer.

SELINA STONE

Trouble is guaranteed

'In this world you will have trouble. But take heart! I have overcome the world.' (v. 33, NIV)

The stadium was filled, and the people were applauding. 'God heals all our diseases!' a man exclaimed as a wheelchair-user stood up and walked a few paces. 'Just claim your healing in the name of Jesus!' I was a teenager, watching a well-known faith-healer far below me on a big stage. I raised my eyebrows because even then I knew that healing doesn't come to all. A decade later, I'd contracted a debilitating autoimmune illness and had become a wheelchair-user myself. Despite countless prayers for my healing, I am still not better.

Often people in church want to skate over the uncomfortable hardships of life – sickness, poverty, mourning – because we prefer a picture of God who gives us health and happiness. It's less messy. This is why, perhaps counterintuitively, this is one of my favourite promises. Jesus himself, just before he went to the cross, guarantees us trouble and suffering in this world. Whenever we're tempted to think that God has abandoned us because our life has gone wrong, or we're scattered like the disciples were after Jesus' death (v. 32), or we've been rejected by our church community despite loving God (vv. 1–2), or we're still grieving, despite Christians claiming we should be joyful, we know from Jesus that tragedy and rejection are to be expected. In this world, it's the norm, not the exception, and it doesn't mean we're forgotten by God.

This in itself is a comfort, but Jesus then goes on to make a further promise: he has overcome the world (v. 33). The disciples would be persecuted and eventually die, as we all shall. But it is not the end of the story: we have eternity with Christ to look forward to, where there will be no sin, sickness or suffering. Thanks be to God.

Lord Jesus, you knew rejection and betrayal from those who should have loved you. You experienced heartache and physical suffering. May we not be surprised when trouble comes but look to you for help and hope. Amen.

TANYA MARLOW

A knock at the door

'Here I am! I stand at the door and knock. If anyone hears my voice and opens the door, I will come in and eat with that person, and they with me.' (NIV)

I wonder what would happen if we heard a knock at the door, knowing it was Jesus? Would we throw the door open and invite him in, unreservedly? Would we crack it open a little and suggest he came back when we'd tidied up? Or not answer at all?

I once had a dream in which I was sitting with Jesus in a downmarket café. He asked me if this was what I wanted. Then, we were in a beautiful restaurant, with thick pile carpets and white linen on the table. It was set for two. Jesus handed me a basket of bread and, as he did so, his sleeve rolled back and revealed nail prints in his wrists. It was a powerful vision. It was also a beautiful promise.

This verse, found within the letter to Laodicea, is a picture of Jesus knocking on the door of the heart. If we hear his voice (John 10:16) and respond to that gentle knock, he will come and 'make [his] home' with us (John 14:23). Once we have opened that door, he promises to be with us 'always' (Matthew 28:20). But he won't force his way in; he waits to be invited.

The best way to maintain a friendship is to spend time with the other person – sharing a meal is a lovely way to do this. But this picture of divine companionship doesn't end when the evening is over; it's a promise of a constant, intimate relationship.

Laodicea was a wealthy church, yet Jesus told them they were poor – they were 'lukewarm' (v. 16). It can be so easy to stop listening to that quiet voice of love, as we live our busy everyday lives. Let's make it a priority to spend time with Jesus today – the one who loves us best.

Can you imagine what it would be like to eat with Jesus? What would you say? What might he say? Spend some time thinking about that.

SHEILA JACOBS

Peter, a life transformed

Alianore Smith writes:

I don't know about you, but in my mind, the Peter we read about in the gospels and Acts seems to be a million miles away from the words of Peter we find in his letters.

In 1 and 2 Peter, he coins various phrases that likely formed your discipleship, whether you realise it or not. He's the one who refers to our 'living hope' in Jesus (1 Peter 1:3, NIV). He writes about how we should 'always be prepared to give an answer… for the hope that you have' (1 Peter 3:15, NIV). He calls the church 'a chosen people, a royal priesthood, a holy nation' (1 Peter 2:9, NIV). His words have gone down in history, inspiring and encouraging Christians across the world for centuries.

And yet, the Peter we meet in the gospels is hotheaded. He acts first and thinks later. He is passionate and honest and vocal. He frequently finds himself in perilous situations. And – of course – he's perhaps most remembered for his vehement denial of Jesus. Journeying with gospel-Peter is an absolute rollercoaster.

Peter in Acts is similar, but all those things about him that seemed in the gospels to be flaws – or at least 'interesting' character traits – are suddenly used to great effect for the building of the church. Peter's passion is unyielding. He doesn't ask for permission to talk about Jesus; in fact, he does it even when he's explicitly told by the authorities *not* to. He continues to find himself in perilous situations, but somehow also manages to get out of them, often in miraculous ways.

If you can, before we begin our journey through Peter's life, take some time to read all the way through 1 and 2 Peter. Bear in mind those measured, passionate, faith-filled words to churches across the region as you read about Peter in the gospels and Acts.

And be encouraged – be encouraged that when we journey with Jesus, our personalities don't change. If we, like Peter, started off passionate and impetuous, we're probably always going to be that way. We're just going to have the privilege of using it for God's glory. We see similar with Saul/Paul: first, he's zealous in persecution, then he's zealous in evangelism.

Peter is a deep encouragement to us all: no matter who we are, no matter how much we think we've messed up, no matter how much of a 'loose cannon' we might appear to be, God can use us mightily for his kingdom and his glory. May it be so.

Called

So they pulled their boats up on shore, left everything and followed him. (v. 11, NIV)

If you work in marketing, you'll be familiar with the rule of seven. That's the theory that a prospective consumer needs to be exposed to a message at least seven times before they'll act off the back of it.

We've probably all experienced it, scrolling social media or noticing ads on public transport: the first time, you don't care about the product or item. But by the seventh or tenth time, you're thinking that maybe you actually *do* need that pair of trousers, new eye cream or new novel.

The rule of seven tells us that as humans we take a lot of convincing to part with our money or change our opinion on something. Turns out, though, the rule of seven doesn't apply when you're confronted with Jesus.

From this account of Peter being called by Jesus, there is no sense that he has met Jesus before. Perhaps he had heard of his teaching, but as far as we're aware, they have never met. And yet, by the end of the morning, Peter has left everything and followed Jesus. What changed?

Jesus wasn't known for his compelling brand. He didn't have a PR team. Sure, the miraculous catch of fish is *quite* the marketing tool, but still… he had only his very essence – his convicting teaching and his miraculous power.

There is something about Jesus and his knowledge, his power, that makes Peter fall on his face, woefully aware of his own sin. There is something about Jesus that astonishes and convicts, that demands we sit up and pay attention – even the very first time we meet him. Peter couldn't ignore it. Neither could James and John. May we, too, find ourselves captivated by Jesus once again.

Think back to the first time you met Jesus – perhaps as a child, or maybe reading the gospels. What made you want to engage further? Thank God for his convicting power, and pray that others would experience the same.

ALIANORE SMITH

Walking on water

**Then Peter got down out of the boat, walked on the water and
came towards Jesus. But when he saw the wind, he was afraid and,
beginning to sink, cried out, 'Lord, save me!' Immediately Jesus
reached out his hand and caught him. 'You of little faith,' he said, 'why
did you doubt?' (vv. 29–31, NIV)**

What point in this story do you stop relating to Peter? I'm pretty sure we
can all understand and empathise with the disciples' (including Peter's)
fear at someone walking towards them on the lake. Perhaps we can even
relate to Peter's declaration: 'If it's you, tell me to come to you on the
water' (v. 28).

I think our imaginations and sympathies begin to flounder a little as
Peter gets out of the boat and takes his first steps on the water. What is
he thinking? The boat is a 'considerable distance' from the shore, and it's
being 'buffeted by the waves because the wind was against it' (v. 24). This
is no swimming pool.

But out of the boat Peter gets, and he starts his progress towards Jesus
when suddenly, human rationality and logic kick in again. He saw the wind,
and he was afraid.

I find it fascinating that Peter had enough faith in Jesus to get out of the
boat – surely where most of us would find our courage lacking – but in the
face of fierce winds and large waves, that's when he crumbles.

How often in our lives do we ask God to lead us to places where we
must trust him, and follow him there willingly, before looking around and
realising that we are scared?

The comfort of this message comes in verse 31: 'Immediately Jesus
reached out his hand and caught him.'

Even when we have had courage to get out of the boat and walk a few
steps, even when we have realised that we are scared, even when our
faith falters, Jesus reaches out to catch us. His mercies are sure. He can
be trusted.

---

*Listen to the song 'Oceans' by Hillsong Music. Consider the words and, if you
feel able to do so, use them as a prayer. Praise God that he can be trusted
even in the midst of a stormy sea.*

ALIANORE SMITH

To whom shall we go?

'You do not want to leave too, do you?' Jesus asked the Twelve. Simon Peter answered him, 'Lord, to whom shall we go? You have the words of eternal life. We have come to believe and to know that you are the Holy One of God.' (vv. 67–69, NIV)

Do you ever find Jesus' words difficult? His teaching hard to swallow? His commandments challenging to obey?

If you do, you're in good company. Today, we meet Peter in a moment of astonishment and confusion. Jesus has just claimed to be 'the bread that came down from heaven' (v. 41) and informed a large crowd that 'unless you eat the flesh of the Son of Man and drink his blood, you have no life in you' (v. 53). This is – in the words of the disciples – 'a hard teaching' (v. 60).

It would be a strange enough teaching today, but when you remember that there is a clear Old Testament prohibition around ingesting blood, you can understand why the Jewish listeners – and Jewish disciples – were particularly offended. The Torah says that anyone who partakes in the blood of any flesh 'must be cut off' (Leviticus 17:13–14), but now Jesus is saying that if you *don't* drink his blood, 'you have no life in you' (v. 53). No wonder people left. No wonder many disciples 'turned back and no longer followed him' (v. 66). But the twelve – including Peter – remain. Why?

Peter puts it simply: 'To whom shall we go? You have the words of eternal life' (v. 68).

Do you relate to Peter in this moment? Have you discovered the sheer, unparalleled beauty of Jesus? Have you realised the truth of what he brings?

When we are confronted with some of Jesus' more difficult teachings – especially in the face of today's culture – it can be easy to want to pack it in, to turn back and to no longer follow him.

But when we realise the reality of Jesus' words and character – his truth, his kindness, his faithfulness to his promises – it is impossible to go anywhere else.

To whom should we go? He has the words of eternal life.

Take some time reflecting on some of the commandments of Jesus which you find particularly difficult. Bring them to God in prayer and ask him for the faith to utter Peter's words wholeheartedly once again.

ALIANORE SMITH

Upon this rock

**Simon Peter answered, 'You are the Messiah, the Son of the living God.'
Jesus replied, 'Blessed are you, Simon son of Jonah, for this was not
revealed to you by flesh and blood, but by my Father in heaven. And
I tell you that you are Peter, and on this rock I will build my church, and
the gates of Hades will not overcome it.' (vv. 16–18, NIV)**

One of the things I always want to know about Jesus' discussions with or
declarations to people is: how do they respond?

Obviously, in some passages we read of people's responses – just yesterday we read of the hearers' confusion about Jesus' words. But in today's
passage, we get no sense of Peter's response to Jesus' remarkable declaration. Was Peter proud? Was he scared? Did he have follow-up questions?
I know I would have.

But we don't get to be privy to any of those. Instead, Jesus' declaration is followed up by a promise: 'The gates of Hades will not overcome it'
(v. 18). No matter what happens, Jesus says, his church will not fall. Those
who follow him will not be defeated.

I wonder how much Peter clung to those words in the following years –
through his denial, Jesus' death and resurrection, Jesus' ascension, and
right into the miraculous growth – and subsequent brutal persecution – of
the church.

As Peter was challenged, imprisoned, flogged and even executed – did
he ever doubt Jesus' words? Or did he draw strength from them amid pain
and fear? When it felt like the church was buckling under the weight of
pressure and persecution, when he was being led out to die, how many
times did he call this promise to mind?

We don't know the answer to these questions. But what we do know
is the fact that we are here, today, reading Jesus' words and journeying
through Peter's life, worshipping in communities and speaking about our
faith, is proof that Jesus' promise has held up.

As they always do.

---

*Listen to the song 'Build Your Church' by Elevation Worship and Maverick City
Music. Use the lyrics as a prayer for places where the church is persecuted or
floundering. Praise God that his church will not fall – no matter what.*

ALIANORE SMITH

Denial

But Peter declared, 'Even if I have to die with you, I will never disown you'… Then Peter remembered the word Jesus had spoken: 'Before the cock crows, you will disown me three times.' And he went outside and wept bitterly. (v. 35 and v. 75, NIV)

Is there something you very specifically regret? A moment that, when you think about it, your stomach clenches and your heart is filled with shame?

We all know what regret feels like – whether it shows up immediately (like it did with Peter) or appears over a period of a time, growing deeper as you learn more about the consequences of a particular action.

Our own experiences with regret are why it's so easy to empathise with Peter in this story – Peter, so bold and ambitious in his declaration of loyalty, just a few hours later so passionate and unwavering in his denial. He denies Jesus three times – the first of which is akin to a formal, legal oath. This is serious denial. And the regret, we're told, is instantaneous.

But that instantaneous regret, theologian Tom Wright points out, is 'the main thing that distinguishes him from Judas in the next chapter – Peter's tears, shaming and devastating though they were, were a sign of life. Judas' anger and bitterness led straight to death' (*Matthew For Everyone*, SPCK, 2009).

Peter's deep and bitter remorse – although painful and perhaps even crippling at the time – shows something profound: Peter had not fully turned his back on Jesus. There was still hope.

It can be easy to seek to avoid regret, to justify ourselves and make excuses rather than acknowledge where we have failed and where we are cross with ourselves for the decisions we've made or actions we've taken. In this story, Peter is to be admired – he acknowledges the pain of regret, and is able to fully express remorse and, eventually, receive forgiveness and a new commissioning from Jesus himself.

Regret leads to repentance. Repentance leads to restoration. Praise God for his unfailing power.

Consider something that you regret or feel shame about. Really dwell with it. Consider if and how you can make amends – bring it before God in prayer and ask for his wisdom, as well as his forgiveness where necessary.

ALIANORE SMITH

Resurrection

But they did not believe the women, because their words seemed to them like nonsense. Peter, however, got up and ran to the tomb. Bending over, he saw the strips of linen lying by themselves, and he went away, wondering to himself what had happened. (vv. 11–12, NIV)

Have you ever let someone down and been desperate to make amends? I remember a time when I broke my mum's favourite mug and simply *longed* for her to get home so I could admit my culpability and receive her forgiveness. Perhaps you have had a similar – or even more intense – experience.

The last time we heard of Peter in Luke's gospel was back in chapter 22, when he denied Jesus. And – in a detail completely unique to Luke's account – we read that after he has denied Jesus for the third time, 'The Lord turned and looked straight at Peter' (22:61). Can you imagine the shame Peter must have felt? He goes outside and weeps bitterly. Even worse, Peter has no chance to make amends, to offer an apology, to express regret and receive forgiveness, because Jesus is executed hours later. For all Peter knows, that's the end of the story. He thinks he must live with that burden, that guilt, for the rest of his days.

Except.

Except, three days later, news: Jesus is alive.

The news – from women, who at that time were not accepted as reliable witnesses in a court of law – is astounding. And so, Peter runs. Confused and questioning though he is, perhaps he is holding on to the tiniest bit of hope that he will have the chance to apologise, to make it up to Jesus.

The good news of Jesus' resurrection is not just true for Peter. He is not the only one who is able to make amends, who is able to change the trajectory, to repair relationships. We all now have that opportunity.

So let us run to the empty tomb in hope, to discover that Jesus is alive – and everything has turned on its head.

Is there anyone you need to apologise to or make amends with, or someone to whom you need to offer forgiveness? Take some time praying about it and ask God for the opportunity and the courage to take the next step.

ALIANORE SMITH

Commissioned

When they had finished eating, Jesus said to Simon Peter, 'Simon son of John, do you love me more than these?' 'Yes, Lord,' he said, 'you know that I love you.' (v. 15, NIV)

Do you ever marvel at God's way of marking key moments in our lives in unexpected ways?

Today's reading is a bookend in Peter's interactions with Jesus. Three(ish) years previously, Peter met Jesus over a miraculous catch of fish after a hard night yielding little reward. And now, years – and so much change – later, Peter is back in the boat and Jesus appears again, telling him to throw his net on the other side. Lo and behold, 'they were unable to haul the net in because of the large number of fish' (v. 6).

So Peter gets out of the boat – another throwback to an earlier adventure – and swims to Jesus. Perhaps, as we considered yesterday, he was desperate to make amends. Perhaps he just needed to see with his own eyes once again the reality of the resurrection. Perhaps it was all of the above (and more). I guess we'll never know.

It is here, as Peter perhaps experiences déjà vu from his initial calling, that Jesus offers Peter the chance to receive forgiveness. Three questions correspond to Peter's three denials. Three commands are given. Peter has not been written off; he's been recruited.

Peter is invited back into Jesus' mission. Peter, who thought he'd blown it. Peter, the denier. Peter, the regretful. Peter, the forgiven. Peter, the shepherd.

'Feed my sheep', Jesus says. Another moment of déjà vu, perhaps. Jesus had been clear that 'the good shepherd lays down his life for the sheep' (John 10:11).

We don't know if Peter knew what he was agreeing to. We don't know if he had any inkling of what lay ahead. But we know that Peter loved Jesus. We know that Jesus commissioned Peter. And we know that when Jesus commissions, he remains faithful – to the very end.

Do you worry that God might have written you off? Are you scared of what your calling might entail, or whether God will remain faithful? Bring these concerns to God – be assured of his forgiveness, and his faithfulness.

ALIANORE SMITH

To Samaria... and beyond!

Then they gathered round him and asked him, 'Lord, are you at this time going to restore the kingdom to Israel?' He said to them: 'It is not for you to know the times or dates the Father has set by his own authority. But you will receive power when the Holy Spirit comes on you; and you will be my witnesses in Jerusalem, and in all Judea and Samaria, and to the ends of the earth.' (vv. 6–8, NIV)

What do you consider to be 'the ends of the earth'? Now, get your phone out and look at Jerusalem on a map. This is where the disciples were when Jesus promised them that they would be witnesses to him 'to the ends of the earth'. Zoom out on the map. How many zooms out does it take for you to see the UK? How many before you can see the Americas or Australia?

When Jesus said that the disciples will be his witnesses 'to the ends of the earth', we don't know what places came to Peter's mind. They most likely didn't even know the island that is now the UK existed – let alone the Americas, Australia or New Zealand.

I, for one, would have had a lot of follow-up questions for Jesus. But before the disciples could even open their mouths, Jesus is taken up into heaven. An act which probably raised even more questions.

Sometimes Jesus promises things or tells us things which are beyond our wildest imaginings. Often, as he does so we have more questions than answers. Peter and the disciples couldn't possibly imagine how far the good news of Jesus would reach. There were only eleven male disciples (Judas, of course, had recently died) and a handful of faithful female followers of Jesus at this point. And their message was going to reach the ends of the earth? How could that be possible?

But we know – because we ourselves are proof of it – that Jesus was right. Peter and the disciples were indeed witnesses of Jesus 'to the ends of the earth'. Because of their faithfulness, their passion and their obedience to the Spirit of God, billions have come to know Jesus and been saved.

Praise God, who works miracles far beyond our greatest imaginings.

Go back to the map app on your phone, close your eyes and navigate to a random country. Spend some time praying for that country, that God would move powerfully and people would come to know him in that place.

ALIANORE SMITH

Speaking up

Then Peter stood up with the Eleven, raised his voice and addressed the crowd: 'Fellow Jews and all of you who live in Jerusalem, let me explain this to you; listen carefully to what I say…' Those who accepted his message were baptised, and about three thousand were added to their number that day. (v. 14 and v. 41, NIV)

How do you feel about public speaking? Is the spotlight (real or metaphorical) something you thrive under, or would you much rather be off stage, perhaps serving refreshments, or engaging one-to-one with people?

We don't know how Peter felt about public speaking. Until this moment, we've never seen him address a crowd. Remember, Peter was a fisherman, so he wasn't exactly a trained orator. And the last time someone asked him publicly about whether or not he knew Jesus, he had vehemently denied it, turned tail and ran.

But then the Holy Spirit appears. By the power of the Spirit, Peter and the rest of the disciples find themselves speaking in all kinds of tongues, proclaiming the 'wonders of God' (v. 11). Accused of being drunk (which I feel is fair play from the crowd, to be honest!), Peter stands up to correct them.

I wonder how Peter felt at this moment. Were his palms sweaty? His legs shaking? His heart racing? Or was he so utterly convicted by God's power and filled with his Spirit that he didn't even notice? Or maybe it was a bit of both – often, when God calls us to do something, he doesn't make us any less scared, he just makes us braver.

Peter's courage and obedience to God's direction meant three thousand people heard and accepted the truth about Jesus' death and resurrection. Even with sweaty palms, shaky legs and a racing heart, obedience to God led to miraculous change.

That's still true today – even when we are afraid, obedience to God's call on our lives can result in something miraculous.

Listen to the song 'You Make Me Brave' by Bethel Music. Bring some of your discomforts and fears to God and ask him to give you courage to be obedient – even when it's scary!

ALIANORE SMITH

27

Sanhedrin

The apostles were brought in and made to appear before the Sanhedrin to be questioned by the high priest. 'We gave you strict orders not to teach in this name,' he said. 'Yet you have filled Jerusalem with your teaching and are determined to make us guilty of this man's blood.' Peter and the other apostles replied: 'We must obey God rather than human beings!' (vv. 27–29, NIV)

Growing up, were you a teacher's pet or more likely to bend (or break!) the rules? Now, as an adult, what's your response to authority more generally?

Today, we meet Peter in a bit of a pickle. He and the other apostles have been told not to preach about Jesus, but they continue to do so. Why? They tell us in verse 29: 'We must obey God rather than human beings!'

Peter has been told by the authorities not to do something. But God has been clear in his directions that they must preach the gospel and the good news of Jesus Christ. What would you do?

Personally, I don't know if I'd have the courage to obey God rather than human beings, especially if – like Peter and the apostles – I was under threat of punishment, torture and even death. But I hope and pray that I would. I hope and pray that, were that choice ever to come to me, God would give me a Spirit of fearless obedience to his word.

Are there things in your day-to-day life where you feel the nudge of the Spirit to obey God rather than humans? Perhaps it's something relatively simple like being honest at work when you're encouraged to lie or 'fudge' something. Maybe it's offering to pray with someone even if it's not the 'done' thing. Or it could be challenging a culture of condemnation and blame with kindness and respect – or sharing the gospel with those curious to hear it.

Whatever it is, we can trust that when we are obedient to God's call, and seek first his kingdom, he will be with us.

Spend some time in prayer, asking God to help you identify areas in your life where you are more likely to listen to humans than to him. Ask for courage to do as he asks – even if it comes at a cost!

ALIANORE SMITH

Dorcas

In Joppa there was a disciple named Tabitha (in Greek her name is Dorcas); she was always doing good and helping the poor. About that time she became ill and died… Peter sent them all out of the room; then he got down on his knees and prayed. Turning towards the dead woman, he said, 'Tabitha, get up.' She opened her eyes, and seeing Peter she sat up. (vv. 36–37 and v. 40, NIV)

I think we all know a Dorcas. The woman – or man, but if we're honest they're often a woman – who just quietly gets on with incredible ministry in the background. Quietly, faithfully loving those the world has forgotten – making tea, wiping tears, serving and blessing and changing lives in a really practical way.

Dorcas is an unsung heroine. She is likely one of many such women in the early church, but it's because of Peter's visit to her home, after her death, that her name is remembered down the centuries. If this Dorcas is anything similar to the Dorcas-like characters I know in today's church, she'd probably be mortified if she knew she had gone down in biblical history for her acts of quiet service.

Peter sees the gaping hole her death has left in the lives of the widows of Joppa – women who were likely living on a shoestring and for whom Dorcas' care could well have been the difference between life and death. Peter sees this and knows that God has not abandoned them. He sees that Dorcas is a faithful disciple, so he calls on the power of God to resurrect her.

And resurrect her he does.

Of course, one day, Dorcas will die again – and she will leave another massive gap. But for now, this story tells us something important: women matter. Quiet, faithful, behind-the-scenes discipleship and care for those in need matters. God sees those to whom we minister – and he sees us as we do it.

God delights in quiet faithfulness. May we do the same.

Think of a Dorcas character you know – in your church or your life more broadly. Take time today to thank them, maybe with a card or a small gift, or just a simple word or message. Pray God's blessing on them as you do so.
ALIANORE SMITH

Gentiles

So when Peter went up to Jerusalem, the circumcised believers criticised him and said, 'You went into the house of uncircumcised men and ate with them.' Starting from the beginning, Peter told them the whole story. (vv. 2–4, NIV)

When was the last time you shared your testimony? Whether in full or in part, the power of story in sharing the gospel is not to be underestimated.

Peter's experience in this passage is testament to that. He's facing some weighty accusations from a group within the church who believed that he had betrayed sacred laws by communing with Gentiles over food. Associating with the uncircumcised over food was strongly discouraged, and Peter had done that by hanging out with Cornelius (Acts 10).

And so, Peter must give an account of his actions – explain himself in front of some deeply suspicious leaders. What does Peter do? He gives voice to his experience – he gives his testimony of God at work, God speaking to him by his Spirit.

Sometimes, we simply have to explain ourselves: state the facts, witness to the experience, share our testimony – in whatever form that might take. Whether we're faced with concerned friends, sceptical fellow-believers or actively hostile enemies, there is power in the sharing of testimony.

As we do so, we – like the Jerusalem believers and Peter himself – must be anchored in prayer and humility, rooted in the scriptures, but also open to the movement and guidance of the Holy Spirit.

God still speaks today – in line with what he has revealed in scripture and not diverting from his previous actions in history. We know that by his Spirit and through our testimonies, God is at work in the world.

How can we share our experience of his powerful presence with those around us today?

This week, look for an opportunity to share some or all of your testimony with someone – friend, colleague or curious counterpart. Pray that God would use it for his glory.

ALIANORE SMITH

Escape

So Peter was kept in prison, but the church was earnestly praying to God for him… Peter motioned with his hand for them to be quiet and described how the Lord had brought him out of prison. 'Tell James and the other brothers and sisters about this,' he said, and then he left for another place. (v. 5 and v. 17, NIV)

If you're really, completely honest with yourself, do you think your prayers make a difference? Or think of it this way: if you're in a difficult situation, and you hear that someone is praying for you, are you comforted? Do you believe it will materially change the situation?

Today's passage reminds us that prayer works. Prayer changes things. Peter is in prison, guarded by 16 soldiers. He's likely chained to two soldiers as he sleeps, and his cell is being watched by sentries as well. He's trapped. Peter must have felt helpless. The church must have felt powerless. The whole situation must have seemed almost impossible. And yet…

In verse 5, we read that 'the church was earnestly praying to God for him'. In the face of a seemingly impossible situation, the church did the one thing the church can always do: it prayed. Earnestly. To God. For Peter.

I wonder if Peter knew that the church was praying. I wonder if that brought him comfort. We don't know. What we do know, however, is that things changed. Things changed so dramatically that Peter thought he was dreaming (v. 9). Things changed so dramatically that when Peter appeared at the house of the believers, Rhoda the servant was so surprised she forgot to let Peter in! What a delightfully human response from Rhoda.

Then Peter disappears into hiding. We don't know where he goes. All we know is that the prayers of God's people saved his life in that moment. When confronted with a seemingly impossible situation, God's people prayed, and the miraculous happened.

Prayer works. In big situations and small situations, prayer changes things. Whether we are the pray-er or the prayed-for, we can take great comfort in – and challenge from – that beautiful truth.

What seemingly impossible situation can you pray for today, in faith and with hope that God will work a miracle? If you can, make a note of what you're praying for and the date. Keep praying until something changes.

ALIANORE SMITH

A living hope

Praise be to the God and Father of our Lord Jesus Christ! In his great mercy he has given us new birth into a living hope through the resurrection of Jesus Christ from the dead, and into an inheritance that can never perish, spoil or fade. (vv. 3–4, NIV)

Having journeyed with Peter through Acts, we know that Peter was no stranger to persecution. But we also know that he was no stranger to hope. In fact, in the opening words of this first letter – written to the church in Roman provinces experiencing profound persecution for their faith – Peter is explicit about the source of his (and their) hope: it is Jesus' resurrection.

Peter says that when we come to know Jesus, we are born again into a 'living hope' (v. 3). This is not hope that we cling to as a last resort, that may or may not hold. This is not hope that could wobble should things move or change, or circumstances become difficult. This is a *living* hope. It is sure and certain. It is a hope that is linked to an inheritance that 'can never perish, spoil or fade' (v. 4).

How can we know this? How can we be certain that this hope and this inheritance will not change? Because it is 'kept in heaven' for us (v. 4). Because it has been bought and sealed by Jesus Christ himself.

In our lives today, like plenty of Christians around the world, we may not be strangers to persecution, suffering, even death. But, like Peter, we are also not strangers to hope.

No matter the persecution, no matter the attacks that may come, no matter the pain or the suffering, Peter is clear: as Christians, our hope is *alive*. Our inheritance is secure. Nothing – not one single thing – can change what Jesus has done for us on the cross and through the resurrection.

Praise be to the God and Father of our Lord Jesus Christ! He has given us new birth into a *living* hope.

Father God, I thank you that because of you, we are not strangers to hope. Thank you that our hope is alive, and our inheritance is secure – because of who you are and what you've done. Amen.

ALIANORE SMITH

Hosea: God's redeeming love (part 2)

Helen Williams writes:

Since we last looked at Hosea, we have walked together through Palm Sunday into Holy Week and on to celebrate the resurrection on Easter Day. We have lived through the return of Jesus to heaven at Ascension and celebrated the coming of the Holy Spirit, as promised, at Pentecost. Today is Trinity Sunday, when we celebrate the unity of God the Father, Son and Holy Spirit. But today we also return to Hosea and to the story of the agony of God the Father over his wayward child, Israel.

We left Hosea at the end of chapter 3. Somewhat frustratingly, we don't hear anything more about the prophet and his wife Gomer, but you can be sure that the pattern of their marriage forms the foundation of the rest of the book. The only other reference to Hosea the man comes in chapter 9, with the suggestion that, together with other prophets like him, he has been ridiculed, attacked and rejected for his prophecy.

Chapters 4 to 14 divide into two sets of warnings and accusations, each of which concludes with a passage about God's mercy and of hope for the future. I'm sure you know, but I will warn you all the same, that these chapters are tough. They are full of real tirades of judgement and lots of condemnation of cult prostitution and idolatry. There is punishment, retribution, deep frustration and anger. We see sin in all its depravation and what Paul calls 'the wages of sin' (Romans 6:23) in their unequivocal harshness. But while it's easy to write this off as the response of the Old Testament God, knowing that Jesus has come to save us from this sin, it's also a real wake-up call to us in so many ways. The final verse at the end of the book exhorts the reader to really pay attention if they're wise and discerning, because God's ways are right. His covenant commandments were set in stone for very good reason.

As a tiny bit of fascinating background, it may help to remember that Israel at this time was the northern kingdom (sometimes known as Ephraim) and Judah the south. The capital of Israel was Samaria and that of Judah, Jerusalem. It's a challenging read, but may you meet the God of love in these pages.

All rise!

Hear the word of the Lord, you Israelites, because the Lord has a charge to bring against you who live in the land: 'There is no faithfulness, no love, no acknowledgment of God in the land.' (v. 1, NIV)

As chapter 4 opens we are witnesses to a courtroom scene. God has a charge to bring against his people and here, as chief prosecutor, he presents his case. There are three significant ways the Israelites have broken the binding covenant they made with him at Mount Sinai – namely, in regard to faithfulness, love and acknowledgement of him. These themes recur again and again in the remaining chapters. Here God alludes to how the Israelites have broken at least five of the ten commandments (the third, ninth, sixth, eighth and seventh) as he describes (through Hosea) the breakdown of society with its 'cursing, lying and murder, stealing and adultery' (v. 2), not to mention endless bloodshed. This was not how it was meant to be, and there is a price to pay for unfaithfulness.

Of course, our televisions, radios and newsfeeds reveal many of the same problems lying at the heart of our world now. Even the land, both then and now, is in mourning. On the one hand, there is death because of drought and hunger, and on the other, animals, birds and fish are often literally 'swept away' in floods (v. 3). Did Paul have these verses in mind when he wrote to the church in Rome describing the 'groaning' of creation as it waits for its future liberation (Romans 8:22)?

I'm struck by God's exhortation to 'know' him and by the fact that not knowing him is a punishable offence. The Hebrew word, *yada* (to know), describes a personal relationship rather than just an intellectual knowing. I remember a speaker once saying to church leaders: 'Your congregations don't want to hear clever things about God; they want to know that you know him.' I've never forgotten that. It's relatively easy to know 'about' God, but does my face shine, like Moses, with the brightness of knowing him?

'We continually ask God to fill you with the knowledge of his will through all the wisdom and understanding that the Spirit gives, so that you may live a life worthy of the Lord and please him in every way' (Colossians 1:9–10).

HELEN WILLIAMS

Pop Idol

'They have exchanged the glory of God for the shame of idols... They
ask a piece of wood for advice! They think a stick can tell them the
future! Longing after idols has made them foolish.' (v. 7 and v. 12, NLT)

When my kids were young, we used to love watching *Pop Idol* on Saturday
night, especially pleased when a Christian boy got to the final of one series!
This word 'idol' has become acceptable to us. People often talk of their
music, sports or media idols. I even found myself saying to a friend the
other day that I've become idolatrous about my grandson – always thinking of his needs, of toys and clothes I could buy, of when I will next see him.
While this may not seem very serious, I was shocked at myself. Anything
that takes over my thinking, that I obsess about or that demands an overwhelming amount of my time is in danger of taking God's rightful place.

God has some pretty serious things to say to his people about idolatry,
and it seems that no one, not even priests, is exempt from his accusa-
tion – in fact, you would be a hypocrite if you were to blame others and
not yourself. The thing is that they had 'exchanged the glory of God for the
shame of idols.' Through the desert years, they had begun to understand
his passionate love for them, to experience his daily leading and provision,
to see his magnificent glory. In the easy, prosperous years of the promised
land, they had forgotten, started to be intrigued by local gods and idols,
and begun to join in with elaborate rites around their worship. In fact, they
had taken all the abundance God had provided and attributed its provision, and dedicated its wealth, to Baal and other Canaanite deities.

It may seem a million miles from where we are today, but it may be
good to ask God if there is anything in our lives which we are in danger of
worshipping.

---

*God's first two instructions for life: 'You must not have any other god but me'
and 'You must not make for yourself an idol of any kind... You must not bow
down to them or worship them' (see Exodus 20:3–5).*

HELEN WILLIAMS

The lion king

'I will be like a lion to Israel… I will carry them off, and no one will be left to rescue them. Then I will return to my place until they admit their guilt and turn to me. For as soon as trouble comes, they will earnestly search for me.' (vv. 14–15, NLT)

You know how it feels when you're trying to get a vital message over to someone who doesn't quite get it – you find yourself falling over yourself trying to explain, offering new angles, different images, anything to hammer the message home. After the courtroom summons, this chapter brings us to God's verdict. You can hear his desperate love for, frustration with and judgement of his people as the similes and metaphors pour out of his mouth. He accuses them of being like prostitutes and thieves and says they will become like rubble. He warns that his anger will be like a waterfall; that he will destroy them as a moth destroys wool. They will be like rotting wood and like sick people without a cure. Finally, he says that he, the lion, will tear them to pieces and carry them off to his lair.

This message is full of hints of the imminent invasion of Israel and Judah by the great superpower, Assyria. There will be devastation and ruin, despite the fact that Israel has tried to ingratiate itself with Assyria and seek its protection. God knows the people will ultimately come with their sacrifices to plead for mercy but utters these devastating words: 'They will not find him, because he has withdrawn from them' (v. 6).

In the verse, though, something happens. It's as if God takes a long, slow breath and says sadly, 'You know they *will* realise their guilt, their misery, the emptiness of life without me, and they will not only look for me but do so, in desperation, with all their heart'. There is a glimmer of hope that, as the father of the prodigal son searches the horizon for him, God will see his people turn in penitence and will race towards them to embrace them.

God waits patiently and will never force us. He operates on a wholly different timescale from us. As Peter says: 'He is patient with you, not wanting anyone to perish, but everyone to come to repentance' (2 Peter 3:9, NIV).

HELEN WILLIAMS

Love me do

'Come, let us return to the Lord. He has torn us to pieces but he will heal us; he has injured us but he will bind up our wounds… Let us acknowledge the Lord; let us press on to acknowledge him. As surely as the sun rises, he will appear.' (v. 1 and v. 3, NIV)

The interjection of Hosea's own words come as a welcome relief in this chapter, after the bitter charge God has brought against his people. He presents the extraordinary possibility of hope, healing, revival and restoration. It's hard for us to grapple with how God can be both wounder and compassionate healer, but we need only to look forward 750 years to see the one who was 'pierced for our transgressions' (Isaiah 53:5) stumbling towards the horror of the cross. There on the cross he would bear our sins 'in his body… so that we might die to sins and live for righteousness; "by his wounds you have been healed"' (1 Peter 2:24).

But we need to turn – to turn and return to him. We also need to 'acknowledge' (or know) him. 'Press on to acknowledge him' (v. 3), urges Hosea. What might that look like for you today? Is there a new way God might be wanting to reveal himself to you in the days ahead? Ask him, beg him to show you how you can get to know him and his will better. He has made a way for us through the cross, we have only to acknowledge him, and he will come to us, bringing the refreshing living water Hosea speaks of.

We looked on Sunday at the recurring exhortations of this book – to be faithful, to love and to acknowledge God. Now, continuing his exasperated plea to his people, God asks: 'What can I do with you?' It's the agonised cry of every parent at some point in their child's life, and it highlights the fleeting nature of the people's love. It's a beautifully poetic description too: 'like the morning mist, like the early dew that disappears' (v. 4), but what an indictment and what a challenge for each of us.

How often have I started a day with you, Lord, only to forget to acknowledge you again within moments of leaving home? I really do want to love you better. Help me to stay connected to you throughout today. Amen.

HELEN WILLIAMS

Toast

'When I found Israel, it was like finding grapes in the desert; when I saw your ancestors, it was like seeing the early fruit on the fig tree. But...' God will reject them because they have not obeyed him; they will be wanderers among the nations. (v. 10 and v. 17, NIV)

God says his people are toast! Their hearts burn like ovens; their passions are like flaming fires; they're even like a flat loaf that's burnt on one side (7:4–8). He's done with them. He actually mocks them, saying they're like an old man who doesn't realise his hair is turning grey (7:9), a dove who will be trapped (7:11–12), a faulty bow (7:16) and a wild donkey (8:9). Through chapters 7—10, God's agony is writ large on each page. In heart-breaking contrast, he paints the poignant picture of when he first drew his people into relationship with him as he rescued them from the terrors of Egypt and led them to the place of covenant in the Sinai desert. It was like 'finding grapes in the desert', he reminisces, 'like seeing the early fruit on the fig tree' (9:10). You were a 'spreading vine' (10:1), he says, full of fruitful promise.

What we actually see in these chapters is a nation set apart for something really special, but so easily deceived, choosing to integrate, undiscerningly, with other nations and to ingratiate themselves with Assyria – basically putting their hope and trust in anyone other than the God who'd promised to save and lead them. Through Moses, God had said 'choose life' (Deuteronomy 30:15), but they had chosen to walk away. So, we see the exodus tragically being reversed: 'Ephraim will return to Egypt' (9:3), God says. If you have time to read chapters 7—10, you will see that the beautiful promised land will gradually return to a wilderness. Thorns and briars will take over the abandoned land and the people of Israel will be back to wandering around the wilderness (9:17). What an unmitigated disaster!

I'm reminded of God's rebuke to the Ephesians (Revelation 2:4–5): 'You have forsaken the love you had at first. Consider how far you have fallen! Repent and do the things you did at first.' Lord, rekindle our love for you.

HELEN WILLIAMS

Learning to walk

It was I who taught Ephraim to walk, taking them by the arms; but they did not realise it was I who healed them. I led them with cords of human kindness, with ties of love. To them I was like one who lifts a little child to the cheek, and I bent down to feed them. (vv. 3–4, NIV)

My daughter frequently uses an emoji of a broken heart in her texts, often in response to a cute video of her nephew (also my grandchild) doing something for the first time! He gets around very efficiently on his bottom, this boy, but we're all helping him learn to walk, encouraging him to use a little trolley or trike. So I feel very tuned in to these opening verses of chapter 11. This is a brokenhearted father, remembering the precious moments of early childhood.

The picture of the father is so tender, so patient, taking the time to lead, to support, to heal, to feed and to lift that child to his cheek in pure love. This always brings a tear to my eye. I wonder, if we truly understood even half of this parental love God has for us as individuals and as a worldwide Christian church, how this would impact our lives, our worship and our influence on the world.

The very powerful thing here is that God remembers. Remembering was written into the Passover following the exodus: the people were always supposed to remember God's mercy and liberation. They forget, but God remembers and, in his remembering, his 'heart is changed' within him (v. 8). There's the suggestion that the original Hebrew word used means 'overthrown'. Yahweh's own sense of himself is renewed. 'I will not … for I am' (v. 9). He cannot condemn his children to eternal damnation and separation. Instead, he roars like a lion, calling his children home and, tremblingly, home they come. 'I will settle them' (v. 11), he says. The very heart of God is love, kindness, compassion, welcome and hospitality.

Whatever your experience of being parented, spend some time allowing God to bend down and lift you, as it were, to his cheek. He is the lion who roars, but he is also the most gentle, affectionate of fathers.

HELEN WILLIAMS

Re-turn

Return, Israel, to the Lord your God. Your sins have been your downfall! Take words with you and return to the Lord. Say to him: 'Forgive all our sins and receive us graciously, that we may offer the fruit of our lips.' (vv. 1–2, NIV)

In chapters 12 and 13, Hosea shares three stories of God's faithfulness and Israel's rebellion: those of Jacob, Moses and Saul. Time and space preclude our looking at them now, but if you're able, do read those chapters – they are inspiring parts of the salvation story. They culminate in 13:14 with the shout, 'Where, O grave, is your destruction?', the verse which Paul quotes in his great resurrection passage in 1 Corinthians 15. God reminds his people that he is their Saviour, their one true King.

I remember the moment I first really understood this verse. I was sitting with my younger brother as he was dying some years ago. I knew that, tragically, Stephen was going to die, but he was so sure of his eternal destiny and already we had a genuine sense of heaven. We realised that ultimately death had no power.

And now to the glorious climax of this extraordinary book. Chapter 14 begins with the instruction, once again, to 'Return' – this word which is used 22 times in Hosea. Re-turn! Turn from your distractions and turn towards God. Hosea suggests how this might be done – 'Take words with you', he says, and ask God to forgive your sins and 'receive you graciously'. I love this idea of taking words with us into God's presence, almost like a criminal preparing a confession. He goes on to say that this is so that God may be worshipped and reinstated in his rightful place as king; that the false security placed in others may be renounced, and that God's fatherly love and goodness may be embraced.

God's response to this, his song of restoration, is just beautiful. Do read it now in verses 4–8 and hear God speak it over you, perhaps inserting your name where appropriate.

We've only been able to skim through Hosea over this past week and back in March. It's a hard-hitting (and sometimes positively mystifying) book, but do take a moment to ask God what he might be highlighting for you today.

HELEN WILLIAMS

Sermon on the mount: living out God's kingdom

Fiona Barnard writes:

On my shelf is a book of speeches which, it is claimed, have 'changed the world'. They include addresses from politicians, campaigners and activists. They are rallying cries, condemnations of social 'ills', justifications for certain actions, attempts to persuade doubtful listeners. They were made for inaugurations, beginnings, wars, grief, national struggles and farewells. They have captured a mood, convinced a crowd, clarified a position, misled a generation, birthed a soundbite. Significantly, Jesus of Nazareth is the first entry with two texts from the sermon on the mount: the beatitudes and the Lord's Prayer. Indeed, for many, the sermon on the mount is the essence of Christianity, with its ethical ideals and principles for religious practice.

There are parallels in Jesus' ministry with that of Moses, signalling continuity and newness. Both come out of Egypt, leading people to the realm of promise through water and wilderness. As Moses goes up the mountain to the presence of God and descends with God's law, so Jesus teaches from a mountain concerning the law's fulfilment through him. Both bring deliverance from bondage. Both offer a vision of salvation. Both shape a community for God. Notably, this sermon is not directed to those who admire Jesus, but primarily to those committed to following him. It presents the transformed attitudes of new covenant disciples described in the beatitudes, as they are liberated from cycles of anger, violence, unfaithfulness, materialism and deceit. It shows their character and behaviour under the rule of God in relationships, and shows integrity, generosity and prayer.

How refreshing is this panoramic vision of the reign of God in practice! Today, we are awash with vacuous rhetoric: self-interested promises of politicians, dubious sales pitches of dealers, aspirational talks of those we cannot trust. By contrast, Jesus' manifesto reveals an everyday faithfulness more subversive, more far-reaching, more socially transforming, more life-giving than any speech limited by historical or geographical context. As you reflect on this sermon, be encouraged: Jesus is less concerned with what you must do, and more about what God does in you as you seek him first.

Solid blessing

'Blessed are the poor in spirit, for theirs is the kingdom of heaven. Blessed are those who mourn, for they will be comforted. Blessed are the meek, for they will inherit the earth. Blessed are those who hunger and thirst for righteousness, for they will be filled.' (vv. 3–6, NIV)

I glanced down at my feet and the sky flashed by. I looked up and glimpsed a shifting street. As the great wheel whizzed me round, nothing was in the right place. This was no thrill. I could not wait for the fairground ride to be over.

A quick scan of the beatitudes can leave us with a similar feeling of disorientation and discombobulation (I love this word!). We are presented with a mosaic of people who are 'blessed', or, following other translations, 'happy': the poor in spirit, those who mourn, the meek, those who hunger and thirst for righteousness, the persecuted and insulted. There is something unsettling about it. The cynical may question the inclusion of the pure in heart and the peacemakers, for they rarely have a comfortable life since they are often at odds with the majority. Furthermore, the second part of each statement seems to dismiss present misery with the promise of future blessedness: 'they will be comforted… inherit the earth… be filled… see God…' What is Jesus saying?

A longer gaze at these words reveals God's radical ways. Tom Wright translates 'blessed' as 'wonderful news': here we see beautiful countercultural hope for a broken society. In Jesus' coming, God breaks into a world of godless strutting, where the powerful hoard pleasure and privilege. Theirs is the glitzy fairground which is soon gone. In Jesus' kingdom, those who know they need him and humbly weep for their sins, who are desperate for his righteousness and return mercy to others, who single-mindedly seek him and work for peace, experience deep satisfaction. Those whose priorities reflect Jesus' values, and who suffer for it, can be certain of a joy which begins now and never ends. Jesus' rule is like the solid ground I longed for on that crazy fairground ride.

'You're blessed when you get your inside world – your mind and heart – put right. Then you can see God in the outside world' (Matthew 5:8, MSG). How do you react to this and the other beatitudes?

FIONA BARNARD

Job description

'You are the salt of the earth. But if the salt loses its saltiness, how can it be made salty again?... You are the light of the world... let your light shine before others, that they may see your good deeds and glorify your Father in heaven.' (vv. 13, 14 and 16, NIV)

'What am I going to do with my life?' I wonder when you last heard those words – perhaps from a teenager overwhelmed by choice or a job seeker uncertain about her skills, perhaps from a career-weary friend or even from your own heart. Sometimes in my prayers for guidance, I recognise I want God's green light as insurance against failure. I discover he doesn't work that way. I suspect his guidance is much broader and more life-giving than I imagine.

In these earthy, domestic images, Jesus throws the options wide open. He calls us to be who we are: salt and light. This is his challenge: 'Just as salt prevents food decaying and heals wounds, be those who stop the rot in the world. As salt brings flavour to a meal and makes people thirsty for pure water, get out of that salt cellar and scatter yourselves in an unsatisfied society. Just as light brings safety, comfort and knowledge, so people don't trip, so they can see each other's faces and their own situation clearly, so they can work together and know where they are going, shine with my light. Reflect me in your everyday lives.' Any role, whether salaried or not, that stops the rot and shines Christ's light of truth and love is surely a great way to spend your life and will bring honour to your Father in heaven.

A Christian doing research in a hospital told me how many of her interviews with busy nurses happened as they washed out bedpans together (before they were disposable!). There she heard about their struggles and worries. To her surprise and delight, she discovered God was using her as welcome salt and light in a most unlikely place.

'You're here to be salt-seasoning that brings out the God-flavours of this earth... You're here to be light, bringing out the God-colours in the world' (MSG). Ask God to enable you to be who you are in him today.

FIONA BARNARD

Rules and right living

'Don't suppose for a minute that I have come to demolish the Scriptures – either God's Law or the Prophets. I'm not here to demolish but to complete. I am going to put it all together, pull it all together in a vast panorama.' (v. 17, MSG)

'Stay at home. You cannot visit your grandmother. Don't leave town. You must wear a face mask.' Pandemic lockdown rules were astonishing in their specificity and reach. So too was the outrage when those who made and announced the laws were caught breaking those rules. It highlighted the fault lines between those who obeyed the rules and those who imagined that instructing others was sufficient. Knowing the urgency of keeping communities safe did not always translate into changed behaviour.

'What is the point of the Old Testament?' I hear people ask. 'It is just a bunch of outdated rules and weird preachers shouting at people for not obeying them. I just stick to Jesus, nice and simple.' Only it isn't. Here, as he paints vibrant word pictures, the law and the prophets are central on Jesus' kingdom canvas. They describe the character and community of a God-reflecting people. His life interprets, illustrates and illuminates all the Father's longing for a beautiful relationship of trust. Where God's people have failed by disobeying, manipulating or fixating on only some parts, Jesus fulfils God's will completely. He also secures reconciliation for those who trust in him.

The other day, my Muslim friend Mariyah, new to life in the UK, presented me with a copy of the Koran. 'In our religion, we cannot drink or eat pork. We must pray five times a day,' she stated. 'Do Christians have rules to obey?' My head raced with images of very ungodly liberty in our society, which rightly shocks her, alongside true freedom offered in Christ. This sermon helped me explain how Jesus honours the law by taking us to a deeper level with it, working its demands into our very hearts and attitudes.

How would you have replied to Mariyah? For you, what captures the dynamic of being both a willing slave of Jesus and his friend?

FIONA BARNARD

Shouting at the TV

'You're familiar with the command to the ancients, "Do not murder."
I'm telling you that anyone who is so much as angry with a brother or
sister is guilty of murder… Thoughtlessly yell "stupid!" at a sister and
you are on the brink of hellfire. The simple moral fact is that words kill.'
(vv. 21–22, MSG)

'I don't like her haircut. It makes her face very fat. And goodness, what
an idiotic thing for an "expert" to say!' Watching the television is rarely a
passive activity with me. I never thought much about it until I spent nine
months praying through Ignatius' *Spiritual Exercises* under the guidance
of a spiritual director. It was a brilliant experience of walking with Jesus,
imagining myself present at different events in his life, recognising my deep
God-given desires and seeking to respond to his kingdom call. It was also a
time of uncovering habits and attitudes which stop me from being totally
free to follow Jesus.

Spending such a long time in prayer, digging deep, unearthed many
surprises. One of them concerned my dialogue with the TV. I realised that
my tendency to have an opinion on the appearance, manners, words or
character of individuals on screen betrayed a critical superiority. While
it did not hurt them, it exposed my ugly heart and mindset. It offended
God in whose image they had been made. It gave me regular practice for
extending my judgementalism to those around me.

So when I read these words of Jesus, I get what he means. It is so easy
to justify irritation or resentment when we have to deal with imperfect
people! But murder does not come from nowhere. It is a matter of the
heart, long before a finger pulls the trigger, whether showering bullets
or words. It is 'justified' when other people are unkind and selfish. It is
fortified by fault-finding and keeping scores. It is bolstered by anger and
resentment. It wrecks lives and communities. I may not be a killer, but I am
part of the domino effect of social discord. My worship is rendered empty
and meaningless.

---

*Where in your heart does anger or criticism lurk? Ask God's Spirit to search
you and cleanse you.*

FIONA BARNARD

Guarding eyes and heart

'Remember the Scripture that says, "Whoever divorces his wife, let him do it legally…?" Too many of you are using that as a cover for selfishness and whim, pretending to be righteous just because you are "legal"… In making your speech sound more religious, it becomes less true. Just say "yes" and "no".' (vv. 31–32 and vv. 36–37, MSG)

Confession time: when it comes to rules, I am a wriggler. I feel I can judge for myself if the law is a good one, and if it isn't, I give far too much attention to considering how I can get out of obeying it. I reword or interpret it from a different angle. Alas, it seems I am not the only one. These words of Jesus are directed at those whose attitude to the law was, 'What can I get away with?' Jesus calls out lust and lies for what they are.

At a time when women could not own property or have careers, marriage was not a romantic choice, but an economic necessity for survival. Jesus is concerned about wives becoming destitute through the advice of religious leaders which benefitted only husbands: 'Here's what to do if you have got your eye on another girl and want rid of the one you've got. It just takes her to burn your dinner or nag you. You can get yourself a divorce certificate and you are done.' Many of us know the heartache and damage across families when a marriage is a twisted means of selfish desire rather than being based self-giving love.

Along the same lines is the issue of fiddling with the truth. Pious teachers sanctioned dishonesty if you swore by heaven or earth or your head, the equivalent of crossing your fingers behind your back, as a means of getting out of it. Jesus is straight: 'This is an outrageous manipulation. God cares for integrity. Show that people can trust you.' In the complexity of family relationships, there is so much collateral damage from self-interested behaviour. Cultural practices may vary across the centuries, but Jesus' words uncover the heart issues which are timeless and right up to date.

Bring before Jesus someone you know who is struggling in a painful relationship. Ask him for his eyes and heart to pray for them.

FIONA BARNARD

Love as hard as nails

'If someone drags you into court and sues for the shirt off your back, giftwrap your best coat and make a present of it… You're kingdom subjects. Now live like it. Live out your God-created identity. Live generously and graciously towards others, the way God lives towards you.' (v. 40 and v. 48, MSG)

Recently, as I was chatting to a fellow patient in hospital, she disclosed cherished memories of attending church and told me she kept a Bible by her bed. 'What does Jesus mean to you?' I asked. She replied: 'He is pure unconditional love, he loves everybody.' Spot on. Jesus is so very attractive: tender towards the brokenhearted, concerned for the sick, generous to the hungry, fun with children. You may be able to recall occasions when you too have experienced his gentle kindness, perhaps when you least deserved it. So everything in you cries, 'Jesus, I want to be like you.'

Soon we realise it's a challenge. Christ's charismatic love, illustrated in the beatitudes, has a razor-sharp strength to it which defies fluffy sentimentality. Meekness and mercy and mourning, purity of heart and peacemaking and the pursuit of righteousness are not for the faint-hearted. In a violent, selfish world, they invite insults, mocking, persecution and martyrdom. This is what lies ahead for Jesus. It is also what awaits his friends.

You can't accuse Jesus of not telling it like it is. Love means not taking revenge into my own hands but leaving it with God. It means not only tolerating those who are cruel or unlikeable, but actually praying for them and seeking their well-being. It means not limiting generosity to friends but embracing strangers and even enemies. I realise I like 'unconditional love' when it applies to me and in a vague way to pleasant humankind, but when it confronts my tendency to protect myself or demand justice or opt for a comfortable life, I find it hard. And yet, this too is beautiful, radical. It is just what this world needs, just what the Father looks like and just what God's Spirit promises to shape in me if I will let him.

Spend time basking in the warmth of God's gracious generosity to you. Then consider these words: 'Love your enemies. Let them bring out the best in you' (v. 44). What is the challenge for you in these words?

FIONA BARNARD

Audience of one

'Be especially careful when you are trying to be good so that you don't make a performance out of it. It might be good theatre, but the God who made you won't be applauding… God doesn't require attention-getting devices. He won't overlook what you are doing; he'll reward you well.' (v. 1 and v. 18, MSG)

I was walking down the main street, when I came upon a man from my church whom I had just seen at a prayer meeting. He was chatting to a woman with a begging bowl. I joined them, knelt on the pavement and listened to her lengthy story. After we parted, a question haunted me: 'Would I have stopped if that Christian man had not been there?'

Religion and good works tend to come as a pair. It is obvious why: faith finds expression in care for others. However, it can also be a lethal combination. The temptation to be seen, admired and commended can be both subtle and irresistible. We do it without realising. We also collude with this myth that we can always judge spirituality from a superficial observation of words and actions: 'You are so godly. You pray like an angel,' or, 'You are such a spiritual giant. How you manage to take aid overseas, sit on dozens of committees and still have time to do shifts at the food bank I'll never know.'

Have you ever considered how many of the great works of God are done away from human gaze? Take creation, for example, and Jesus' birth, his life between the ages of 12 and 30, his prayers to the Father, the moment of resurrection – God does not have an ego to stroke or people he wants to impress. Likewise, Jesus urges his followers to limit their intended target audience to one: to God himself. In prayer, in fasting, in feeding the poor, their focus is to please him. It is his appraisal, his smile, that matters.

Lord, thank you for your Spirit's hidden, transforming work in me! As I live for you today, may I bring a smile to your face. May I look to you alone in trust and gratitude. Amen.

FIONA BARNARD

Simply pray

'Our Father in heaven, reveal who you are. Set the world right; do what's best – as above, so below. Keep us alive with three square meals. Keep us forgiven with you and forgiving others. Keep us safe from ourselves and the Devil. You're in charge! You can do anything you want!' (vv. 9–13, MSG)

We all pray at some time in our lives, don't we? Recently I embarked on an exploration of the Lord's Prayer with a group of international students. Most knew little about Christianity but were interested in matters of faith. Prayer seemed a good starting point, common as it is to many religions. It was fascinating to observe how they compared their understanding with these words Jesus taught his friends.

They seemed unfamiliar with God being personal, like a kind father. A number viewed prayer as wishful thinking, expressed to no one or, at most, an undefined force of nebulous character. The possibility that every person could be known by a loving creator was something they had not really considered at all. They were surprised at the practical aspects of prayer, at the invitation to ask for what they needed each day. In a mindset where money and hard work gets them what they want, daily dependence on a God they could not see seemed very foreign and unnecessary. A couple physically jumped when I suggested we could pray that political leaders might govern with God's kingdom values; they could not imagine prayer actually making any difference in the world.

So now as I come afresh to this simple framework for prayer which Jesus gave us, I am awed by the privilege that is mine, that is ours. As we lift our eyes in worship to our Lord, we celebrate his kingdom and align ourselves with his values. We come to a personal God who knows us intimately. He welcomes us and wants us to express our reliance on him for our needs. He wants us to keep returning to him for forgiveness and protection, knowing that we will go deeper into his generous embrace. What an immense privilege is ours!

Pray the Lord's Prayer slowly. Let it frame your time with God. Include pauses to add things you would like to say to him. Imagine him listening attentively.

FIONA BARNARD

You choose!

'The place where your treasure is, is the place you will most want to be, and end up being… If you open your eyes wide in wonder and belief, your body fills up with light… You can't worship two gods at once… Adoration of one feeds contempt for the other.' (vv. 21–22 and v. 24, MSG)

Choice can be overwhelming: a restaurant menu that reads like a short essay, a hundred TV channels offering a vast array of mediocre entertainment, medical options heavy with hopeful possibilities and worrying side-effects, diary demands and clashes. If you are like me, I waste far too much time weighing up the alternatives and agonising over what I might forego. Sometimes I just cry, 'Simply tell me what to do!'

Here Jesus whittles down the possibilities. He presents three stark choices which will end up directing all our other life options. They concern priorities which do not coexist comfortably. In fact, they pull in opposite directions. 'You decide,' he says. 'Will you focus on material stuff or spiritual capital? On light or darkness? On God or money?' It seems almost too simplistic, and yet it's utterly realistic. When I was learning to drive, my often-terrified instructor would insist, 'You end up steering in the direction where you are looking.' It was true. Several distractions almost ended in disaster. Focus was crucial for road safety.

What we discover as we fix our eyes on Jesus, rather than on making ourselves rich or protecting our successes, is that God's kingdom is spacious. We are not manhandled into narrow asceticism and stiff-lipped living. We enjoy heavenly treasure now in the company of Jesus. We discover our identity and purpose in his business. We share in the priceless delights of community and care. We participate in adventures that no cruise or trek can rival.

'I'm asking God for one thing, only one thing: to live with him in his house my whole life long. I'll contemplate his beauty' (Psalm 27:4). Pray through what it might mean for you today 'to live with him in his house'.

FIONA BARNARD

Look!

'Look at the wildflowers… If God gives such attention to the appearance of wildflowers – most of which are never even seen – don't you think he'll attend to you, take pride in you, do his best for you?… Give your entire attention to what God is doing right now.' (v. 28, v. 30 and v. 33, MSG)

As hospital machines beeped and dripped beside me, I lay staring at the ceiling light for hours. It was all I could do. I'd been struggling to breathe, and the doctors were trying to work out what was wrong with me. I couldn't move or read or pray. Too soon, my mind filled with dark thoughts of death and decay. Imponderable questions about God that make sporadic appearances amid the normal busyness of life now gathered pace like a thunderstorm. I felt terrible.

When I was discharged, still panting, I lay on my sofa. I stared at the flowers my friends had brought me: red and yellow and orange and purple, spiky and silky, buds and blooms, little leaves and longer ones, tall stems and short. Held together in a vase, they rested there, graceful and elegant. As I gazed on them, my heart soaked up the delicate, priceless delight of God's handiwork. Those bouquets spoke of his extravagant artistry and care, his fresh, ever new colourful daubing in nature. 'Look at my flowers,' whispered Jesus to my fragile heart. 'Keep gazing at them. Aren't they magnificent? Know that you are so much more precious to me than them. Will you trust me for today?'

When did you last stop and stare? How long is it since you set aside your to-do list, your worry list, your what-if list, your never-get-round-to-it list, your why list for a while? Might you make time simply to feast your senses on something beautiful God has made and stay with it? Let it refresh your soul. Let it refocus your attention on the one who made you with so much love. Let it reshape your priorities and prayers. For the sake of his kingdom.

'Steep your life in God-reality, God-initiative, God-provisions… You'll find all your everyday human concerns will be met' (v. 33). Take a leaf, a stone or a flower in your hand. Spend time noticing the details. Let it speak to you.

FIONA BARNARD

Stop and search

**'Don't pick on people, jump on their failures, criticise their faults –
unless, of course, you want the same treatment. That critical spirit has
a way of boomeranging. It's easy to see a smudge on your neighbour's
face and be oblivious to the ugly sneer on your own.' (vv. 1–3, MSG)**

When people insist, 'She never said a bad word about anybody', I confess to
feeling mild irritation. In my humble opinion, they are either lying or don't
know her very well. Alternatively, she was not very perceptive and didn't
feel much alarm in the face of injustice. But then, perhaps Jesus' warning
about being judgemental is exactly what I need to ponder.

I guess we can agree that a critical attitude devastates relationships
in the home and workplace, the church and wider community. A person
whose default response is negative exhibits a festering bitterness which
kills fruitful life and creativity. Significantly, Jesus points to the irony
that it can often be an attempt to distract ourselves and others from the
mirror reflecting our own brokenness. However, Jesus cannot mean that
we mustn't discern what is right and what is harmful. He certainly did not
respond blandly to the hypocrisy and callousness of people he encountered. Indeed, he goes on to caution, 'Do not give dogs what is sacred; do
not throw your pearls to pigs' (v. 6, NIV), which at the very least, involves
the use of our critical faculties to work out who are the pigs and dogs as
well as the pearls and the sacred.

As ever, Jesus is intent on transforming our attitudes and motives from
the inside out, saying to us (to paraphrase verse 5): 'Wash yourself first,
recognising your own filth, and then you will be free to wipe others clean.'
This is not a denial of dirty lives but an acknowledgement of dependence
on the ongoing purifying work of the Holy Spirit. I know I desperately need
his wisdom to know when to call out cruelty and inequality in imitation of
Christ, choosing my words with timely compassion and truth, and when to
overlook niggling annoyances, letting silly things go.

---

*'Search me, God, and know my heart… See if there is any offensive way in
me, and lead me in the way everlasting' (Psalm 139:23–24, NIV). Let God
search your heart.*

FIONA BARNARD

Ask for what you need

'If your child asks for bread, do you trick him with sawdust? If he asks for fish, do you scare him with a live snake on his plate?... You're at least decent to your own children. So don't you think the God who conceived you in love will be even better?' (vv. 9–11, MSG)

'Can you teach me how to pray?' Ying whispered to a leader of the Bible discussion she was attending. Christianity was new to her. She was testing to see if it worked. Behind that question were others: 'Are there special words I must use? Are there offerings I should make to a deity? Are there ways I can negotiate a good job, a kind husband, a healthy body, a happy life?' These queries may have begun as very utilitarian probing, but they took her on a much wider quest in the months ahead.

At the heart of Jesus' teaching on prayer is a simple encouragement: come to the God, who is more loving than any earthly father. He wants to give good life-giving gifts, better than insubstantial trinkets that tickle your fancy. So speak to him, not using clever or manipulative language, but with direct child-like requests. And as you return to him again and again to seek this provision, you will be cultivating a relationship of dependence and trust in him. You will enjoy his indulgent generosity.

There will be many times when what you want is not granted. Here you are called to draw on knowledge of God's passionate love for you. You will need to believe, even through tears and tantrums, that he cares too much for you to grant you *everything* you ask. Sometimes it takes the agony of unanswered prayer to make us dig deeper into what we truly desire and need. Precisely because he wants to give us good gifts, God may say 'no' to the slot machine approach to quick fixes. These lifelong lessons can feel like countercultural hurdles. However, as we grow in our love for Jesus, we cannot be satisfied with the snakes and sawdust on offer.

Pause to ask: what is the deeper desire beneath my everyday requests? Bring it before God. And then wait in dependent trust.

FIONA BARNARD

Be fake-aware

'Don't look for shortcuts to God. The market is flooded with surefire, easygoing formulas for a successful life… Knowing the correct password – saying 'Master, Master', for instance – isn't going to get you anywhere with me. What is required is serious obedience – *doing* **what my Father wills.' (v. 13 and v. 21, MSG)**

'I don't know what truth is,' my geologist companion shook her head with resignation. 'Fake news is everywhere.' Somewhat surprised this came from a scientist, I challenged her: 'But surely in your field, with solid rocks, there are some things about which you can be certain?' She shrugged, 'No, academics want to get published, so they will say anything.'

Perhaps humankind has always had a complex and manipulative relationship with the truth. Jesus is very concerned throughout this sermon that his followers' lives should line up precisely with his words which they profess to obey. He warns against taking the easy, popular path in life which promises comfort and satisfaction and success. He urges them not to fall into the trap of accommodating themselves to impressive soundbites which are actually hollow. Otherwise, they will lose their way amid rousing outward show and eloquence. When all is said and done, being a faithful disciple is a challenge in a world of shifting falsehoods. In Jesus' kingdom, integrity is what counts.

Knowing my own heart, I recognise that while I dislike hypocrites, I am well practised in the art myself. I am tempted to look good so that God and the world at large will be pleased with me, and I get the life I crave. So what does it mean to say 'Master, Master' and really mean it? What does 'serious obedience' look like? In a society broadcasting its own fabricated mantras for its multiple expediencies, what does the truth of Jesus say? When brash self-preservation, achievement and charisma appear like tantalising junk food, how does genuine Christ-like character, humility and integrity deliver healthy yields?

Where, in Jesus' words today, is the challenge for you?

FIONA BARNARD

Working words into life

'These words I speak to you are not incidental additions to your life, homeowner improvements to your standard of living. They are foundational words, words to build a life on. If you work these words into your life, you are like a smart carpenter who built his house on solid rock.' (v. 24, MSG)

I am coming to believe that too many sermons are bad for me. Similarly, too many Bible studies and Christian books don't do me any good either! You see, the more I know, the more opinions I air, the more conclusions I reach, the more I can distract myself from the radical need to do anything about any of it. The more I hold in my arsenal as I encounter God's truth, the less I allow it to shape me. Prolonged exposure to the blinding glory of Jesus can make me dash for suncream to protect myself from being burnt by holiness. It's strange really, because I want God's Spirit to transform me, but it's hard work and I am lazy.

So as we come to the end of the sermon on the mount, Jesus presents me with a simple choice: what am I going to do with all I have heard? Will I allow Jesus' challenge to penetrate my well-practised defences? Is there even one thing I will take away? I shake my head at the stubborn learner driver who ignores the instructor's words, at the unimaginative trainee chef who sticks to one familiar recipe, at the foolish builder who dismisses health and safety rules. Because ears, will and heart are not aligned. Will I be different? How will I dig deep foundations of consistent obedience rather than tinker with one 'interesting' teaching and then another?

Visualise some Christians you admire: what is it about them? The ones I appreciate are real flesh-and-blood characters. They are diverse and outward-looking, flawed and humble. There is a grounded simplicity about their devotion to Jesus, a single-mindedness that takes them on risky, self-denying, God-honouring, life-affirming, compassionate paths with him. What a companion! What a life! What an adventure!

What has Jesus underlined for you afresh in the sermon on the mount? What one way might you live this out?

FIONA BARNARD

The creation story

Selina Stone writes:

At the beginning of the Bible, before we read anything else, we are presented with a poetic tale of how creation came to be. In this story, God is the main protagonist, working as one and three. God is present before anything else, as the source of life and reality. We are drawn into an account of God calling into existence what does not yet exist, recognising its goodness and delighting in it. We find God setting rhythms and patterns into creation, which will allow it to keep on going throughout time, with creatures and plants able to reproduce. We learn that people were made in God's image with great care and then given unique responsibility to govern the earth. It is a story which begins with a blank canvas and ends with a masterpiece.

Yet reading the creation narratives is particularly poignant for us, as we live in the reality of an environmental crisis. All over the world, extreme weather events are becoming increasingly common. The natural world, including wildlife, sea creatures and forests, is under threat due to centuries of over-consumption and greed. In many ways human action is undoing the harmonious picture of creation which we find in Genesis. The readings for the next seven days will combine reflections on God as creator and the importance of the created world with thoughts about our own lives as creatures of God. They will be rooted in the scriptures but also engage with the urgent environmental crisis affecting us all.

My hope is that these reflections will allow you to see yourself as part of God's creative expression. Far from being a cog in a machine or an unimportant factor, I hope you will see yourself as made with intention and loving care. But I also hope that you will prayerfully consider what God might be calling you to do and to pray in response to the needs of God's created world. This includes the natural world and its creatures, as well as all people – especially those affected most severely by climate change – and all the systems and structures we have created. In this way we might better fulfil our vocation to govern the earth with integrity and love.

Life in the darkness

Now the earth was formless and empty, darkness was over the surface of the deep, and the Spirit of God was hovering over the waters. (NIV)

Culturally we have been conditioned to see darkness as bad and light as good. Whether in films, in advertisements, in art or in language, we associate what is dark with evil and what is light with what is pure and good and right. And yet right at the start of the creation story we begin with darkness that is full of potential. The darkness is not evil; it is a deep place, waiting undisturbed; it is a place where God's Spirit is pleased to dwell. The image I have of the Spirit of God hovering over the waters is that of a great bird, swooping down to take a closer look, and then flying just over the waters so its wings skim the surface. It is quiet just before God starts to speak.

Both in the world around us and in our own lives, we might experience periods that feel dark. We might try to run away from it but often we cannot; it can surround us or even consume us. The temptation again is to see darkness as bad, something to be avoided where possible. But this passage encourages us first to remember that the same Spirit of God who hovered over the waters before creation is present with us. The Spirit does not simply hover over our lives, but perches right next to us, or even on our heads. God is not afraid of the dark, even if we are – God sees the potential of what might be created out of it. Where we can only see formlessness or emptiness, God sees depth and the beginning of a whole new reality.

Consider for a moment the darkness you may feel is present in the world or in your own life. What might God, who hovers over the waters, have to say to your fears, worries and concerns?

SELINA STONE

Say what you (want to) see

And God said, 'Let there be light,' and there was light. God saw that the light was good. (NIV).

I used to love watching the show *Catchphrase* on TV when I was younger. Images would be revealed a bit at a time as each tile was removed and contestants had to try to guess what phrase each image represented. The host would remind them to 'just say what you see', which was, of course, easier said than done. In this passage we find God doing the opposite – God does not say what God sees; God says what God wants to see. Using all of his creative power, God simply says, 'Let there be,' and there is. God is not afraid of darkness but wants to see light, because God is delighted by light. When he looked at the light he created, we are told, 'God saw that the light was good' (v. 4).

The first thing we learn about God from the Bible is that God is the reason everything exists. God is the source of life, of reality, of the world, of us. And all of it started with a word. There are many different perspectives on the power of our words in our faith. Some believe we have this same power to say things and create out of nothing; others that our words only have power when we use them to pray for God to act. The power of words in how we speak to others and even ourselves is also important to consider. Wherever we stand, what we say and what others say can have a huge impact on our emotions, our mental well-being, our decision-making and on what we create. This passage reminds us of God's creative words and power, and also encourages us to consider the power of our words and the realities we create with them.

Reflect on how you speak to yourself, to God or to others. What emotions, limitations or possibilities are you creating with your words? Where do you need God's words to create something new in your life or the world?

SELINA STONE

Creation care

God said, 'Let the land produce vegetation: seed-bearing plants and trees on the land that bear fruit with seed in it, according to their various kinds.' And it was so. The land produced vegetation (NIV).

Many of us buy our fruit and vegetables from a supermarket, and so we are disconnected from the land and the processes which produce vegetation. As we reach for the nicest looking apples, often wrapped in unnecessary amounts of plastic, we are far removed from the farmer who woke up each morning to nurture the trees, spray the fruits and pray for good weather. This passage brings us right back to basics – that the existence of vegetation, of the wide variety of fruits, vegetables and plant-based products, are all the result of God's creativity and are gifts from God. Not only does God bring vegetation into existence, but he also makes it possible for them to reproduce themselves by bearing their own seeds. It's genius!

This is an important reminder for us as we take account of how humanity has failed to care for the trees and the vegetation God creates in this passage. We have cut down God's trees, drained so much resource from the earth and polluted it to the extent that we are losing so many kinds of plants and vegetation. Our destructive behaviour is undoing the creative work of God. This passage encourages us to repent of our actions, especially those of us in the richer nations of the world which have plundered and drained the earth in the name of development. We might also give special regard to farmers, and those who plant, grow and pick vegetation. Today's reading calls us to reimagine how we might eat, spend money and live if we remember that vegetation, trees and seed-bearing plants were in fact God's idea.

Thinking about your relationship with the land and with the earth, what might you express gratitude for? Is there something you might need to repent of? What action can you take to make it right?

SELINA STONE

Recognising sacred times

And God said, 'Let there be lights in the vault of the sky to separate the day from the night, and let them serve as signs to mark sacred times, and days and years, and let them be lights in the vault of the sky to give light on the earth.' And it was so. (NIV)

Speaking about the stars, the moon, the sun and signs in the sky is often associated with new age spirituality or witchcraft, and certainly there are various practices regarding 'lights in the vault of the sky' (v. 14) which stand in opposition with the Christian faith. However, here we have a clear explanation of why God made the stars, the sun and the moon: to be signs of 'sacred times' and to give light to the earth.

What might 'sacred times' mean? The nativity story gives us one example when the magi see a sign in the stars that leads them to the newborn Jesus. 'Sacred times' could also refer to the seasons and rhythms which God has set within creation: night and day, and spring, summer, autumn and winter. Or it might refer to the festivals and celebrations which took place at set times of the year and had spiritual significance.

This passage can lead us to a deeper awareness of the inherent connectivity of all things. The sun gives us heat and light, and the moon keeps the earth on its axis and controls the tides. But they also have a role in reminding us of God, in helping us to attend to the rhythms that God has built into all of life, including us. These rhythms involve rest and activity, productivity and restoration, coming and going, losing and gaining, leaving and returning. We do not need to worship the sun or moon to acknowledge this, but we can marvel at the intricacy of creation and the lights in the sky, which call us to pay attention to the sacred in our lives and in the world.

As you consider the importance of the sun, the moon and the stars for marking sacred times, do you need to trust God more with the different seasons of your life? Bring this to God in prayerful reflection.

SELINA STONE

Loving God's creatures

God created the great creatures of the sea and every living thing with which the water teems and that moves about in it… and every winged bird … God blessed them and said, 'Be fruitful and increase in number'. (v.21a and v. 22a, NIV)

When we reflect on the story of creation, we can often centre it around ourselves as human beings. Yet time and time again it is made clear to us that so many other aspects of creation are considered good by God. This has nothing to do with them being useful for us, but simply because God has made them. We see this clearly in this passage about the creation of sea creatures, birds and animals. Like all other aspects of creation, God says they are good, but this time God goes further: God blesses all of the creatures, that they might be fruitful, increase and fill the earth. In the beginning, God delights in seeing a wide variety of different creatures filling creation to the brim.

There is a stark contrast between this image of creation full of life and the global problems we now face. Our over consumption of meat and fish, the risk of extinction of certain creatures due to hunting for food or fashion, or environmental destruction all stand in the way of God's blessing being realised for God's creatures. The rich variety and the increase of different creatures are undermined by humanity's lack of restraint. And yet in our own homes, lives and communities, there might be some action we can take to care for God's creatures, especially those at risk of harm and extinction. We might take in rescue pets, or support wildlife conservation charities, or cut down on our consumption of meat, fish and animal products. Actions like these enable us to stand in solidarity with God's creatures who though blessed by God, live under threat of destruction which will impact creation overall for generations.

Lord, we repent of the ways we have stood in the way of your blessing over your creatures through greed and lack of self-control. Teach us to love your creation and to act in line with your will. Amen.

SELINA STONE

God's image, our responsibility

God created human beings in his own image… blessed them and said to them, 'Be fruitful and multiply. Fill the earth and govern it. Reign over the fish in the sea, the birds in the sky, and all the animals that scurry along the ground.' (vv. 27–28, NLT)

We come to the creation of human beings as a continuation of God's creative expression. God's pattern so far has been to create good things, and to sit back after each day's work and say, 'This is good work.' When God creates human beings, we are called 'very good' (v. 31). God sets out to create human beings 'in God's image', a term which has provoked much debate. Since God is spirit, we cannot look like God, but something about God's being has been given to us in the creation process. There is some kind of family resonance between God and us, similar to a child being the 'spitting image' of their parent. For some, the resonance is captured in God asking humanity to govern the earth. All creation is made by God and called good, animals are commanded to multiply and fill the earth too, but only human beings are given the responsibility to 'govern' and 'reign over' (v. 38).

We can take our lead from God the creator as to what governance and reigning should look like. God has reigned over and governed creation by hovering gently, calling forth beauty and wonder, and providing for all he has made. There is no trace of self-serving agendas, domination or oppression. So when we think about our relationship to creation, we should be led in this direction. To govern and reign, as people made in God's image, is to protect, to nurture, to provide for, to care for and to steward with integrity. This includes the natural world, but also our communities, our streets, our collective resources and all that we have made out of what God has made. In this passage we are called to take responsibility, in ways which represent the creator God who said, 'Let us make human beings in our image' (v. 26).

As you ponder God creating humanity 'in his image', how do you feel? What does it mean to you? Ask God what this should mean for you at this particular point in your journey of faith.

SELINA STONE

Godly rest

By the seventh day God had finished the work he had been doing; so on the seventh day he rested from all his work. Then God blessed the seventh day and made it holy, because on it he rested from all the work of creating that he had done. (NIV)

Rest is godly. This is what we learn from this passage. It can seem counter-intuitive in a world which attaches our worth to how much we work and produce, but nevertheless it is true. This is not the same thing as saying laziness is godly – God was resting after labour and creative expression. He stopped what he was doing and took time to reflect on what he had done. And this time of rest was blessed and made holy.

This is an important reminder for us, as we can be tempted to work and never stop. Sometimes this is because of a perfectionist streak. God's creation was declared good and human beings very good, even though humanity would eventually sin and not reflect perfection.

The truth that God is satisfied with creation, including us, is an important aspect of our faith. It should in turn cause us to rest. Striving for perfection to gain approval from others and even ourselves can be exhausting. This can also impact our spiritual lives, as we seek to be perfect to earn God's love. This kind of living is unsustainable and is eventually destructive to our souls, our joy and our peace.

In our spiritual lives, God delights in us being present and recognises our goodness despite our imperfections. God sees his image in us, even when we fail to see it in ourselves or when others fail to recognise it. When we are aware of this, we can enter into spiritual rest, no longer striving for God's approval but receiving God's love, grace and mercy as a free gift. As God rested, so he calls us to rest as we sit with him, reflecting on what is, and spotting the good.

Thank you, God, for teaching us to rest. Help me to lay down the burdens which steal my peace and joy, and to rest in your love for me, despite my imperfections. Amen.

SELINA STONE

How to live simply

Tanya Marlow writes:

Minimalism is getting maximum exposure these days. Interior designers promote clean lines and white walls to make us feel less cramped. Environmentalists beg us to buy organically, seasonally and locally. Wellness coaches tell us we need time out for meditation. Parenting experts say that too many toys overwhelm our children.

What the western world is waking up to is the harm of capitalism and commercialism. Our bodies and minds are not created for overconsumption. We work more hours than we should to earn lots of money so we can buy lots of stuff and then buy bigger spaces to store it all. The end result is chaos, clutter and clamour, and it's exhausting.

Simplicity, choosing to live with neither too much nor too little, has long been a Christian value, particularly lived out in monastic communities over the years. It's a theme that runs throughout scripture, calling on us to be generous with our possessions and time, and not to crave worldly riches. In today's materialistic society, to seek a simple life is a radical and rebellious move that goes beyond painting our walls a peaceful off-white. Living simply does not mean living easily. Living the simple life is hard – you have fewer choices, it gives you less security and it can be very tedious. What it does offer us is focus: space and time to prioritise what is really important.

Due to a decade and more of being housebound with chronic illness, I've been forced to live simply in terms of my time. In my past, I would rush eagerly from meeting to meeting, filling my days with people. Now I can only do one activity a day. It can get lonely, and I still find it hard. However, it has given me focus. When I see friends, I'm truly present and appreciative of the time I have with them.

Over the next fortnight we'll consider all our resources – time and money, especially – and how by living simply we can regain focus and contentment.

One thing I seek

One thing I ask from the Lord, this only do I seek: that I may dwell in the house of the Lord all the days of my life. (v. 4, NIV)

When I first started dating Jon, who is now my husband, we were inseparable (and insufferable). Walking to lectures had been mundane but travelling with him was a delight; washing dishes was a chore until he was there beside me; eating traditional student pasta dinners was now a romantic date. We bent the laws of physics, somehow finding extra minutes and hours in every day. Newly in love, we were obsessed with spending time with each other.

David, though he had many flaws, was similarly obsessed with spending time with God. He became one of the first kings of Israel, with many responsibilities, people to meet and things to do. He could have become a workaholic or a pleasure-seeker, with all the opportunities for work and fun at his disposal. At times, he was guilty of neglecting his duties for pleasure. But David's strength was this: he delighted in the Lord and loved to worship God. The Lord was his light, salvation and stronghold (v. 1), giving him confidence even when facing his enemies (vv. 2–3). He loved God so much he begged to be in God's presence, inquiring of God's wisdom all of his life (v. 4), as though the temple were his home rather than the palace.

This is the difference between Zen Buddhist minimalism and Christian simplicity: its goal. The purpose of Christian simplicity is not primarily to make our life more streamlined; it's to have space to enjoy God, 'to gaze on the beauty of the Lord' (v. 4). The purpose of simplicity is to lose materially in order to gain spiritually. How might this change our attitude to our upcoming week?

Let's imagine our relationship with God is like two newly dating people. How might we discover extra minutes in our day to spend time in God's presence, delighting in God? How can we involve God in our mundane tasks?

TANYA MARLOW

One thing you lack

Jesus looked at him and loved him. 'One thing you lack,' he said. 'Go, sell everything you have and give to the poor, and you will have treasure in heaven. Then come, follow me.' (v. 21, NIV)

My friends Andrew and Sarah arrived at Heathrow airport, hair wild and suitcases flailing, checking they had everything they needed to travel to Sarah's native USA. Triumphantly, they handed over their tickets and passports.

'And your marriage certificate?' the assistant asked. Their faces fell. It was during a Covid pandemic lockdown and all non-US citizens, including Andrew and the kids, had to prove they were related to an American to enter. They couldn't fly without it.

'Does it help if I tell you I know exactly where in our filing cabinet it is?' Andrew offered.

Like Andrew and Sarah, a good man once discovered he lacked one crucial thing. He had been confident he possessed everything he needed to inherit eternal life – blessed by God with riches, he was also very religious. But the close observer would notice that Jesus omitted some of the ten commandments in his list (v. 19) – crucially, worshipping no other gods and not coveting. The rich man thought that he had everything covered. Yet Jesus, loving him, says that he lacked the most crucial thing: the ability to let go of his possessions for spiritual treasure.

Jesus doesn't tell everyone to sell everything, and indeed Jesus' ministry was bankrolled by several wealthy women (Luke 8:3). Jesus does warn, however, that being rich makes it nigh impossible to follow him (vv. 23–27).

For insurance purposes, I once had to list all the individual items I owned, which was a lot. If all my possessions were destroyed in a fire, I would be very sad. But reading this passage, I see Jesus' challenge to me. It's easy for us to get complacent if we are rich and to misinterpret comfort as morality. Jesus still calls us to lose our comfort for the sake of his kingdom.

Try listing all the items you own. What does that reveal to you? How does your attitude to them need to change? Which of your possessions might Jesus be calling you to sell and give the proceeds to the poor?

TANYA MARLOW

One thing God requires

And what does the Lord require of you? To act justly and to love mercy and to walk humbly with your God. (v. 8, NIV)

If yesterday's passage made you panic that God was requiring you to surrender all your belongings, today's passage is a reassurance of why that may be missing the point. When God gave the law to Moses, there was a tightly regulated system of sacrifices to God. Not only was this a worshipful offering, remembering that everything they owned came from and belonged to God – a proportion of what was sacrificed was reserved for those who served in the temple, to keep them fed – it was also affordable: generally ten percent of what a person owned or earned. But some wanted to be extra religious, extra blessed by God and gave more. It was generally the rich who could afford to be showier in their offerings, expecting God's reward.

Here, Micah is exasperated with this and condemns excessive, unnecessary religious sacrifice. God doesn't want 'thousands of rams' or 'ten thousand rivers of oil' (v. 7). Importantly, God definitely didn't want the cruel pagan practice of child sacrifice (v. 7). Similarly, it would be wrong for us to metaphorically 'sacrifice our children'; for example, giving our time volunteering in a soup kitchen but neglecting time with the kids. Rather, the Lord wants general principles of justice, mercy and humility (v. 8) to govern our giving.

It can be tempting to turn living simply into a kind of religious boast. The purpose of simplicity is not to make us look good. Simplicity is for others. We sell possessions and give to the poor because it's important to share society's wealth. We give money sacrificially because suffering people need relief. Looking outwards to others' needs keeps us grounded, or 'humble', as the Bible puts it (v. 8). Act justly, love mercy, walk humbly with our God – this is what Christian simplicity looks like.

'Live simply that others may simply live' (unknown origin). Pray through Micah 6:8 for yourself. One possible application is eating a cheaper meal once a week and donating the difference to a charity alleviating food poverty.
TANYA MARLOW

One thing is needed

'Martha, Martha,' the Lord answered, 'you are worried and upset about many things, but few things are needed – or indeed only one.' (vv. 41–42, NIV)

Confession: I am an anxious cook. When I was well enough to cater for friends coming round, I would get out my recipe books and read them line by line, weighing out the ingredients beforehand. I served my meals an hour after I meant to because the preparation took so long. By the time I sat down with my friends to chat, I felt frazzled and distracted by whether I'd done a good enough job on the meal.

I wonder whether Martha was also a perfectionist, anxious to show hospitality to Jesus and the disciples by cooking up a feast, whereas Jesus came to her house for relationship, not primarily to be fed. Mary recognised the main event – learning from Jesus. In this case, Martha was ironically inhospitable to Jesus by not spending time with him.

We can't know for sure, but I wonder if Martha could have prepared something simpler for Jesus, so she wouldn't have needed Mary's help. So often our lives get more complicated because we're looking to impress people, even subconsciously. We want to serve the best food, hang out with the right people, look well-dressed and have the tidiest house or the best-behaved kids because we want to fit in or impress others. This can also reveal underlying anxiety that we're not good enough for other people. We need to simplify our expectations of ourselves, not to be 'the best' but 'good enough', so we don't miss the main event of enjoying others' company.

As you think about your own attitude to time with family and friends, consider what might be 'good enough', rather than perfect. In life, are you in danger of missing 'the main event'? Is there a way you can simplify your expectations for yourself?

Lord, illuminate my inner perfectionism and anxieties. When I am distracted by chores, help me to see and honour the people around me. When I am choked by the worries of life, may I sit at your feet and receive. Amen.

TANYA MARLOW

One thing I do

But one thing I do: forgetting what is behind and straining towards what is ahead, I press on towards the goal to win the prize for which God has called me heavenwards in Christ Jesus. (vv. 13–14, NIV)

'My postie has a PhD,' my friend Daniel told me. We were sitting in his peaceful Cornwall home. I was surprised. 'But isn't that kind of a waste of his qualifications?' I asked. 'No,' Daniel replied slowly. 'He was in a demanding job, but it was bad for his mental health. Now he has a position where he earns enough to live on, gets exercise every day, and after his shift has enough time to spend the day however he wants.'

Daniel's postal worker had this much in common with the apostle Paul – he was overqualified for the job he was now doing. Paul lists the most impressive Jewish CV possible (vv. 4–6) – he was born into the right kind of society, excelled in his studies and held an impressive position. He also did a little persecution on the side, which won him respect. He had much to be proud of – yet, because of Jesus' death and resurrection, he now does just 'one thing'. Paul looks ahead to the prize of knowing Christ more, rather than looking behind at the social status he's lost (vv. 7–14).

Ambition isn't necessarily bad, but it can disturb our clarity of vision. Sometimes our goals are in harmony with God's call on our life. Other times, our soul feels weighed down by ambitions or split in two directions. We can be envious of others' success. If we lose a dream job, we feel destroyed. We can get so focused on the achievements we desire, whether we reach them or not, that we lose sight of the fact that these mean nothing in comparison with the privilege of knowing Jesus. I love dreaming up lists of goals, but I often forget to put 'knowing Jesus more' ahead of them all. Living simply means living to know Christ.

A question: how might you simplify your ambitions in light of what truly matters? A prayer: Lord, I bring you my goals, ambitions and desires. Sift them, leaving only what you have for me. I want to know you more. Amen.

TANYA MARLOW

The greatest gain

But godliness with contentment is great gain. (v. 6, NIV)

As we've explored the 'one thing's of the Bible, we've seen that we can simplify: our priorities, like David; our possessions, like the good man; our religious worship, like Micah; our expectations of ourselves, like Martha, and our ambitions, like Paul. Now we're moving on to the great taboo of polite society: money.

Paul wrote to Timothy to warn him not to be like other church leaders who seemed to believe God would reward their good work with financial blessing (vv. 3–5). Paul, who now had to work as a menial tentmaker and receive gifts from churches to afford his ministry, knows that God's beloveds are often poor. Although money is not the root of all evil, as it's often misquoted as being, the love of money is the cause of lots of kinds of evil: selfishness, workaholism, oppression of workers or the land, pride, lack of empathy, tax avoidance, greed. Paul's instructions are stark: we are to flee this (v. 11) and save piercing ourselves with many griefs (v. 10).

I'm married to an Anglican minister. Vicars receive a 'stipend', which means they work six days a week and get a large house provided plus enough money to live on, the equivalent of a dental nurse's salary. It's fascinating to me which of our clergy friends describe their condition as either rich or poor, though they all receive the same.

Much of this is about attitude. You can be poor and love money. You can be rich and not realise it. Either way, we reason that we deserve more, without realising we might already have enough. Loving money means resenting what we don't have; living simply means appreciating what we do have. Paul's bar for satisfaction is set low at just 'food and clothing' (v. 8). His challenge to us is to seek contentment, which is the greatest gain.

Loving heavenly Father, I bring my financial worries to you. Provide for all my needs, I pray, and fill me with contentment. Amen.

TANYA MARLOW

Living simply in a time of famine

Your clothes did not wear out and your feet did not swell during these forty years. (v. 4, NIV)

In 2021, my son came down with long Covid, a debilitating chronic illness very similar to Myalgic Encephalomyelitis (M.E.), robbing him of energy. It has no cure. I'd already lived through 20 years of progressively worsening M.E. myself, which has rendered me mostly bedbound, so this was devastating news. It coincided with a downturn in our personal finances. I know many people with M.E. who have spent thousands on private treatments, vitamins and supplements with varying degrees of success. I hadn't done so for myself, but now it was my son's health at stake. Even though I've lived happily on less income in the past, this was the first time I'd craved money, because I was desperate to afford any and all treatments that might heal him.

There are seasons when life is really, really tough. Finances may play a part in that, as it has done for us, but times of illness, grief or other trials can sap everything from us, so all we can do is just survive. I'm aware there will be readers who've had very few difficulties and others whose whole life has been a struggle. Enforced hardship (famine), as mentioned in today's passage, feels very different from choosing to live more simply (fasting) or living with plenty (feasting).

The Israelites had experienced their season of famine in the wilderness. These issues aren't straightforward – after all, many of the Israelites had died. Poverty is terrifying. But God reminds the survivors of how they were looked after, even in the desert. They had boring manna, but enough to live on, and they were clothed and protected by their divine parent (vv. 4–5). During our times of famine, God still cares for us. Even when it's really hard to feel at times, there will be things to thank God for, and we should do so.

Lord, we bring before you our and others' metaphorical times of famine. We also bring those people in the world facing literal famine. Give us and them what we need, just as a parent would. Amen.

TANYA MARLOW

Living simply in a time of feasting

When you have eaten and are satisfied, praise the Lord your God for the good land he has given you. (v. 10, NIV)

Picture the scene: a charming young man takes the woman he's just met back to his house. She gasps in amazement – the space! The views! The lights that come on when you clap your hands!

'But you're so young – and attractive,' the woman murmurs approvingly. 'You're rich, too?'

At that moment, the door opens and an outraged businesswoman demands to know why the man she employed as a house-sitter has let a stranger into her home. It's not his. It was never his.

It's a beloved trope of romantic comedies, but it also warns us about our attitude to riches whenever we live in times of plenty. Moses' sermon to the Israelites contains a warning for when they're in the promised land. There they will feast and lack nothing (vv. 7–9). He warns them against becoming proud, forgetting God (v. 14) and above all fooling themselves into thinking that their comfortable lives are something they've earned, deserved or achieved, rather than a gift from God (vv. 17–18). Moses urges the Israelites to remember where they came from – slavery in Egypt and wilderness wandering – and remember where their riches came from: God.

It's good to remember that God isn't against plenty or prosperity. Times of fasting are often balanced out with times of feasting, and it's not wrong to be enjoying the pleasures of life, as long as we're not exploiting others in so doing. The danger comes when we think we're owed something, or that we inherently deserve that foreign holiday more than the family who can't afford to get away. There are seasons of feasting, and we're encouraged to enjoy – and share – our good things and fun times. But let's remember we're just house-sitters for God's good world. It's not ours. It was never ours.

Lord, please help me to remember that every good thing I have is a gift from you. Please help me to enjoy freely the good times of feasting, thanking you for them all. Amen.

TANYA MARLOW

Living simply in a time of fasting

'When you fast, do not look sombre as the hypocrites do.' (v. 16, NIV)

My friends, let's call them David and Theresa, were not particularly well off, but they were careful with money and had saved up enough to replace their worn-out kitchen flooring. Finally, they had the exact amount, which at the time was £600. That same day, they had a call from a friend whose car was broken and needed £600 to fix. David said, 'We've waited so long…' But Theresa pointed out, 'They have kids – they need their car more than we need a new kitchen floor.' They quietly donated the money and started saving again for the floor.

They fasted from their kitchen flooring to help others in need. When I heard their story, I was really challenged by their significant sacrifice. In general, each of us should live our lives on a path of justice, as Micah instructs us, but there will be seasons when God calls us to give something extra. Fasting means choosing to temporarily live without something materially good in order to gain spiritually.

In Matthew 6, Jesus links together giving (vv. 1–4), prayer (vv. 5–15) and fasting (vv. 16–18), and I think we're supposed to see that connection too: fasting is not only for our own spiritual benefit but also for the needy. Fasting can mean abstaining from food in order to concentrate our intercessions, but it can just as easily be fasting from a treat so we can donate that money to someone in need or fasting from leisure time to serve someone else. It doesn't need to be a big deal (v. 2), nor should it make us so miserable that we feel the need to tell everyone how hard it is (v. 16) – rather, like David and Theresa's quiet obedience, we work in partnership with the Spirit's prompting. And God sees it all.

Loving Father, I want to help the needy, but I don't want unnecessary self-condemnation or guilt. Am I in a season of famine or feasting, or are you calling me to a fast? Please give me the wisdom to know. Amen.

TANYA MARLOW

Caring for creation

The Lord God took the man and put him in the Garden of Eden to work it and take care of it. (v. 15, NIV)

My husband and I are not remotely green-fingered, but one summer we made a foray into the world of growing tomatoes. We bought those big compost bags you find in garden centres, set up canes for the tomatoes to grow up and watered them regularly. I'd heard that talking to plants and touching them helps them to grow, so I whispered to my fledgling plants. I was invested. And the result? Not a single one grew into a full tomato. We decided it would be cheaper to buy them from the shops in future.

It would be nice if that story had a happier ending, considering that part of living simply is having a connection to the land. But it did teach me this: growing food is a painstaking, beautiful process and a gift from the earth.

When God made the first human, their job was to take care of the earth and work it. When God sent the water, it turned the earth into a lush garden (vv. 10–14). There is something so vulnerable and tender about God handing it over to humanity to look after creation.

We carry that commandment today: to care for the earth rather than exploit it. While it might not be possible for most of us to grow our own food, we can show respect for the earth and the workers. Choosing to live simply means honouring God's creation and those who harvest the produce. It's a sacrifice of time and money to buy from local farmers or greengrocers, and it isn't always possible. But even little things, like not taking home the 'get one free' item if it's going to end up in the bin or eating fruit and vegetables when they're in season locally, show God that we take that command seriously.

A challenge: if you eat meat, could you eat it less often and buy free range? What steps could you take to reduce food waste? How can you support food producers who pay their workers well?

TANYA MARLOW

Living simply requires community

**All the believers were together and had everything in common.
(v. 44, NIV)**

My friend told me about the Taizé community, a group of around one hundred 'brothers' based in France, which takes the value of Christian simplicity very seriously. All the brothers work together, accepting no donations and building no capital. They don't own anything but share everything, even their clothes. One brother, who is unusually tall and can't fit in the others' clothing, jokes that he is spiritually disadvantaged because he has to own his clothes.

They base their practice on the first Christian community. Overjoyed by Jesus' resurrection and filled with the Spirit, the believers shaped their lives around getting as much teaching, fellowship and communion with their Christian family as possible (vv. 42, 46–47). It was a just society, since if anyone was needy, someone richer sold property or possessions and gave them the proceeds (v. 45). Like the Taizé brothers, they shared everything they had.

As we've been exploring the principles of Christian simplicity, it may well feel like a lonely burden to carry. But rejecting the western world's obsession with materialism also means rejecting the individualism that accompanies it. God has designed us to be in community, and that's the only way that simple living truly works.

What would it look like if we started conversations in our churches and neighbourhoods about sharing our resources? Does everyone with a garden really need to individually own a lawnmower? What if seven busy families all took it in turns to batch-cook for everyone else one day a week, giving them only one day per week to cook a main meal? What if we 'shared' our families, so bored teenagers could play chess with lonely housebound people? It takes courage to ask and effort to coordinate, but just imagine what such communities could bring. It could change the world.

God the holy Trinity, who lives together in love, please give me the courage and coordination to take small steps in living alongside other Christians in community. Amen.

TANYA MARLOW

Living simply means having margins

Do not go over your vineyard a second time or pick up the grapes that have fallen. Leave them for the poor and the foreigner. (v. 10, NIV)

Renowned chef Josh Eggleton decided during the pandemic lockdown to use his culinary skills for the community and fed many homeless people with free restaurant-quality meals. In 2023, he relaunched his celebrated Pony and Trap restaurant in the Chew Valley, Bristol, with the aim of using it as a headquarters for eliminating food poverty in the south-west of England. He could have just sat back and enjoyed the perks of being a successful restaurant owner, but he says that giving back to people in need is at the heart of what he does.

God is interested in business. Nestled in a list of commandments for holiness comes this important instruction from God. In the Israelites' farming culture, God tells them to avoid total efficiency. They are not supposed to harvest their whole field or vineyard but leave a proportion for others to help themselves to, a practice called 'gleaning' (v. 9–10). God specifically says that this is for the sake of both the poor and migrants (v. 10), with no strings attached. To God, business practices that support people on low incomes are as important as avoiding idol worship and keeping the sabbath.

In a world that says raising profit and cutting costs is everything to better business, Christian business owners should dare to be different and seek to serve the wider community. But it's also applicable to all as a way of life – having margins in our time that give us blank space and breathing room and a chance to serve others. If we don't overwork and over-commit, we have time for reflection, spontaneous conversation with friends and family and hospitality for a lonely acquaintance who needs to chat or a neighbour who needs help. Living simply means having breathing room in our days for the Spirit to work in.

God of generosity, keep me from worshipping the idols of productivity, overwork and exploitation of others. Help me to carve out margins in my use of time and resources so I can serve people in need. Amen.

TANYA MARLOW

Living in refreshing rhythms

He makes me lie down in green pastures, he leads me beside quiet waters. (v. 2, NIV)

All living creatures align themselves to the rhythms of their environment. Studies have shown that birdsong is louder and at a higher frequency in cities because they have to scream over the noise of traffic. We're not immune from this: we adapt our pace to our environment. When we're living alongside machines, raised voices, urgent demands and pinging alarms, our body aligns itself to this environment, and it's a stressful one. We are not created to thrive that way, and a simple life means we need connection with nature for our well-being. Rachel Buxton, of the University of Michigan, reviewed several studies which showed the same thing: when we're hearing the sounds of birdsong or flowing water, settling into nature's rhythm, even for as little as two hours a week, it improves our stress levels, decreases pain and improves cognition.

David sees the call to spend time in nature as an invitation from God to restore his soul (v. 3). God is like a shepherd, who leads us into metaphorical green pastures and quiet waters and is with us in times of darkness. As David spent his youth as a shepherd, with lots of time both in nature and with God, he could testify to this, and it sustained him when he ruled as king.

Western society lives at too fast a past for humans, and we need to slow down, both for our physical health and spiritual health. In God's creation, we can pay attention to the glory of God displayed in the skies, seas and trees. If we're too busy to spend time in nature, we're too busy. Consider how you can reorder your life to realign yourself to the gentle rhythms of God's creation.

A challenge: take some time today to walk to your nearest green space, or play birdsong if that's not possible, and spend some time listening to what God might be saying to you.

TANYA MARLOW

Living simply with Jesus

'Come to me, all you who are weary and burdened, and I will give you rest.' (v. 28, NIV)

Many years ago, when I was healthier, I was trying to move a dining room table by myself. After several minutes it hadn't shifted much but, at this point, it was a matter of pride. I would do it by myself. As my face went redder, still I could only scrape the oak table across the floor. Just then, a strong friend walked in the door, and I admitted defeat. He picked it up and carried it with me, but honestly, he could have lifted the whole thing by himself. It had suddenly become so light to me.

This is how living with Jesus is: the picture is of two oxen sharing a yoke, but one is taking the whole load (v. 30). Jesus invites all who are exhausted to come to him, because he can lighten our burden (vv. 28–29).

As we've seen over the past fortnight, living simply means sacrificing more if we are richer and asking for more if we are poorer, in order to live a balanced life in a just society. This applies to our resources of money and possessions, but also to other resources, like time. But we miss the point if we leave Jesus out of it. In all of this, we work in partnership with God. We lean on Jesus' wisdom, share the resources God has given us and listen to the Spirit's prompting about when we're called to give extra or place our needs before the church.

For anyone who is feeling crushed by the weight of financial crisis, not sure how to pay their bills, body and soul-weary, unsure how to get the time or emotional support you need, please know that the church community is meant to help. Jesus offers comfort and relief, and his word to you is: 'Come.'

Lord Jesus, in times of feasting, may I be thankful. In times of fasting, may I be joyful. And in times of famine, may I lean on you and see your provision. Amen.

TANYA MARLOW

Titus: truth and lies

Sheila Jacobs writes:

It seems that the recipient of this letter was converted to the faith by Paul, who refers to him as 'my true son in our common faith' (Titus 1:4, NIV). We also read of Titus in 2 Corinthians 7:6, where Paul was 'comforted' by his appearance. We get some glimpses of his personality in 2 Corinthians 7:13, reading that Titus was 'happy', having been 'refreshed' by his fellowship with other believers. He was clearly enthusiastic, as well as discerning (2 Corinthians 8:16–17).

These were difficult times, error and false teaching abounded, and God's people needed careful, trustworthy and responsible discipling – just like today. So, Paul is writing quite an intense letter to his 'son' – one that is a picture of concern for the body of believers under Titus' care in Crete. Paul had left his trusted friend there with the task of strengthening the church and putting godly leaders in place. Corruption was clearly rife, and Paul is encouraging Titus to ensure that God's people were well looked after by spiritual overseers who would be faithful to the Lord and to those they were responsible for.

This is a letter about authentic Christian living. It's an encouragement to keep our eyes on the truth, and nothing but the truth! When we know the truth, we can spot the lies. It also gives great advice on what we should look for in those who serve us in positions of responsibility. Sadly, we know of leaders who make mistakes, or we discover that their lifestyle wasn't quite as godly as we may have once believed; some may even swerve off into false teaching.

Dependable, discerning leadership is important; not so that we can put people on pedestals, but because we need good examples of those living for Jesus so that we may emulate them. We need people we can trust in positions of authority in the church so that when we feel the winds of change blowing in from the present culture, we can trust them to know God's will and God's word and make wise decisions.

I hope that as we journey together through Titus we will be challenged as leaders and helped as individuals to keep in step with the Spirit and strengthened to refute error. Let's reflect on our own conduct as we seek to walk faithfully with Jesus, encouraging others to follow him too.

Where truth leads

Paul, a servant of God and an apostle of Jesus Christ to further the faith of God's elect and their knowledge of the truth that leads to godliness. (v. 1, NIV)

This is Paul's mission statement, to further the faith of Christians and to help them know more about Jesus. In that knowing, as their faith grows, they will understand more about how God wants them to live.

Have you found that putting into practice what we know to be right is not always easy? There can be pockets of resistance in our lives. We believe we are growing in our faith, but we still find it difficult to let Jesus take full control. One time, I asked Jesus what he'd like me to do. I felt he questioned me on how *he* lived. I thought about it. I realised that Jesus spent a lot of time with his Father and didn't have his own agenda. I felt uncomfortably challenged to 'go and do likewise'! Giving God the agenda of my life, even daily choices, seemed scary! But as we get to know Jesus more and more, it becomes easier to let go and to trust him. Knowing him – the one who is himself the truth (John 14:6) – leads to godliness, because the more we draw close to the one who loves us, we will want to please him in how we live.

By dying on the cross and rising from the dead, Jesus has brought us into relationship with the Father. We need no longer be separated from God; we have the opportunity to know him and walk with him. Jesus calls us to follow him, and walking with him means choosing his agenda, not ours, every day. Because of Jesus, we have 'the hope of eternal life' (v. 2). Let's ask him to further our faith, to lead and guide us and to give us the power to live for him.

Think of three ways that will help you grow your faith and understanding of the truth, leading to a life that is really pleasing to God.

SHEILA JACOBS

Hold on tight!

Since an overseer manages God's household… he must hold firmly to the trustworthy message as it has been taught, so that he can encourage others by sound doctrine and refute those who oppose it. (v. 7 and v. 9, NIV)

When I was first a believer, some people from a well-known group knocked on my door and my faith wobbled. I believed in Jesus. I'd encountered him and my life had changed, but I didn't understand in any great depth who Jesus actually was and what he'd accomplished when he died on the cross. I started to study with what was then London Bible College (now London School of Theology). I found a new confidence in knowing why I believed what I believed.

When we know the truth, we can more easily spot a lie. When we're confident, we won't be so swayed by other doctrines. That's why it is important to know what it actually says in the word of God – not what we think it says! There are plenty of strange doctrines around that seem Christian; they often deviate around issues of the Godhead or Christ's deity. We know at that point we must politely shut the door or 'refute' in loving-kindness any error that has crept into somebody's thinking.

Often, especially when we are young in the faith, we might hear something we don't understand or a friend might question us on issues around our beliefs, and we find we can't readily answer. When that happens, it's good to be able to go to a trusted leader who can help us understand the truth of God's word more fully. Today's passage speaks of the high standards of living needed in good leadership, and it's quite sobering to read! Our churches need godly leaders who have 'sound doctrine', who can encourage us in our walk with Jesus. There are lots of different 'gospels' out there. Let's make it our aim to hold on tight to what we know to be true.

Are there any issues of faith where you know you're 'wobbly'? Can you talk to a Christian friend or leader about this today?

SHEILA JACOBS

The right fruit

For there are many rebellious people, full of meaningless talk and deception… They claim to know God, but by their actions they deny him. (v. 10 and v. 16, NIV)

I once bought a young fruit tree. The label said it was a pear tree, so I was quite surprised when an apple grew on it! In Matthew 7:16 Jesus says, 'By their fruit you will recognise them.' That was certainly the case with my apple tree.

In today's reading, Paul uses harsh words, but we can feel his passion. In verse 13 he tells Titus to 'rebuke [false teachers] sharply, so that they will be sound in the faith'. It seems the false teachers were disrupting households for 'dishonest gain' (v. 11). If we're 'sound in the faith' we will be able to recognise those who 'reject the truth' (v. 14), even though they might say they are believers. We need discernment!

Here we read of people who 'claim to know God' (v. 16) but deny him by their actions. We can tell a tree by its fruit! If someone is following Christ, they will not deny him by the way they live – even though we all stumble on the journey. Words are cheap; it's easy to say we're followers; but do our lives, the way we speak and act, say something different?

In these days when we have access to the internet, we need to be careful about what we watch and what we hear. What starts off as a thought that doesn't line up with scripture could lead into gross error. Critical, negative talk, deception and division needs to be challenged when we find it at work in our churches. 'The fruit of the Spirit is love, joy, peace, forbearance, kindness, goodness, faithfulness, gentleness and self-control', as we read in Galatians 5:22–23. Let's make sure that this is the fruit we are bearing in our lives: the right fruit!

Read again Galatians 5:22–23. Spend some time with the Holy Spirit, asking him to grow that fruit in you. Thank him that he has heard you.

SHEILA JACOBS

Integrity

In everything set them an example by doing what is good. In your teaching show integrity, seriousness and soundness of speech that cannot be condemned, so that those who oppose you may be ashamed because they have nothing bad to say about us. (vv. 7–8, NIV)

Here, Paul is encouraging Titus to set a good example. He is giving him instructions in how to look after God's people, but importantly, Titus is encouraged to 'show integrity' in his teaching. You can almost hear Paul saying, 'You live it, so teach it!' Titus is instructed to advise men and women, young and old, to live godly lives. But this passage is challenging to read. After all, in our world, not all women are married or have children, so what does it mean for them to be 'subject to their husbands' (v. 5)? Maybe it's about respect – see Ephesians 5:33, where we also find the husband exhorted to love their wife as they love themselves. Similarly, Paul was living in a culture where slavery was acceptable; in that context, he is pointing to the importance of the gospel (vv. 9–10), but we may find these verses hard to read today.

This passage is essentially about setting an example by doing good, whatever the circumstances. But there's always a bigger picture before us. By choosing to do good, we show the world who Jesus is; we are ambassadors for his 'upside-down kingdom'. It's all about the gospel, the good news of God's salvation. Leaders especially need to be people who show integrity and are serious in what they teach; they should be reliable and honest.

Our lifestyle has to be authentic; people can see straight through anything fake. Even if our friends, family, colleagues or wider society don't always agree with what we believe, if they see the love of God living in and through us, and witness a life of integrity, they may well be drawn to ask questions – not only of us, but also of themselves.

Examine your heart! Are you living a life of integrity in your actions, words and witness? Talk to God about any areas of compromise.

SHEILA JACOBS

Stay close

For the grace of God has appeared that offers salvation to all people. It teaches us to say 'No' to ungodliness and worldly passions, and to live self-controlled, upright and godly lives in this present age. (vv. 11–12, NIV)

When I first became a Christian, I was keen to 'work for God'. Later, I realised that the Christian life was about allowing God to do his work in and through me. I began to understand 'grace' – God's free, unmerited, unearned favour. I didn't have to work to gain God's approval. I already had it because I was in Christ.

However, I also realised that to stay close to God and to please him, it would mean surrendering myself – my choices – to him. Many of us could admit to submitting to 'ungodliness' before we knew Jesus. But if we're honest, there are times when we still may be tempted to live less than self-controlled lives in an area we struggle in.

Titus was exhorted to 'encourage and rebuke with all authority' (v. 15). That's what godly leaders do. It's not easy to receive correction, but it can be helpful and ultimately beneficial for us if it's offered in love, and to encourage us towards God's grace.

Is it time to sit down and think again about what Jesus did for us on the cross? The grace of God appeared in the form of Jesus Christ, who died and rose from the dead, validating everything he ever said and making it possible for humans – so far away from God – to find relationship with him. We owe everything to Jesus. Without him, we would be lost, separated from God forever. That understanding should teach us to say 'no' to all that might hurt and offend God and others, out of sheer gratitude and love. We want to stay close to him, don't we? But we need help. Let's cry out for God to fill us with his Spirit, who gives us the strength and ability to live to please him.

Is there an area of your life where you're struggling to live for Jesus? Are you able to talk to a trusted friend or leader about this? Ask God for wisdom and strength, and his will in the matter.

SHEILA JACOBS

Live different

He saved us, not because of righteous things we had done, but because of his mercy… through the washing of rebirth and renewal by the Holy Spirit, whom he poured out on us generously… so that, having been justified by his grace, we might become heirs having the hope of eternal life. (vv. 5–7, NIV)

I've been part of a street evangelism team for a while, and I find some people shy away from anything to do with God. Perhaps their view doesn't align with what we know of him in his word. They may think they need to do lots of 'religious works' to make him happy. Here, however, we read that we're saved by God's mercy and grace; our lives are renewed and empowered by the Spirit. He is generous and merciful! How amazing is it that God has chosen to justify us and to make us heirs to the kingdom? We have eternal life!

No wonder Paul wants to protect that. He gives instructions about how, as God's people, we need to live differently to the ways we lived before (v. 3); it's important to honour our rulers, be ready to do good, not engage in slander, and be peace-loving, considerate and gentle. Engaging in 'foolish controversies' (v. 9) is more than just a waste of time to Paul; it's serious. Division wrecks relationships. Getting involved in controversial ideas and arguments doesn't just distract us from the gospel; it simply isn't helpful for growing friendships or helping anyone into the kingdom. Anyone who is divisive, says Paul, needs to be dealt with severely (v. 10).

Psalm 133:1 says, 'How good and pleasant it is when God's people live together in unity!' In verse 3 of that psalm, we see God 'bestows his blessing' in such circumstances. And Jesus himself asserts, in John 13:35: 'By this everyone will know that you are my disciples, if you love one another.' Let's remember God's mercy and generous grace, available to all who would receive it. Let's avoid discord, and respect each other, so that not-yet Christians might be welcomed into a loving family of believers.

Lord, please help me to maintain unity with other believers – even when I find it difficult! Show me how to share your love with them and with others. Amen.

SHEILA JACOBS

Devoted

Our people must learn to devote themselves to doing what is good, in order to provide for urgent needs and not live unproductive lives. (v. 14, NIV)

There's an intensity about the whole of this letter, but the final words give us a glimpse into Paul's heart – which is for 'our people' to 'devote themselves' to doing good. Earlier, we read of Paul stressing the importance of the gospel message to Titus; devotion follows on from understanding the gospel and growing in faith (see 3:8).

I sometimes look back at my life as if standing on a hill, viewing a valley. Some of what I see has been productive. Some – maybe not. Ultimately, God will be the one who decides what has been useful for the kingdom (1 Corinthians 3:12–13).

Devoting ourselves to doing good, providing for those in need and not living wasteful lives – these are the instructions Paul is giving not only to the first believers, but also to us. In verse 13 he talks about two people setting out in mission; the Christian community should ensure they had all they needed.

It has been well said that if we are believers, we are all in 'full-time Christian service' – even if we are not missionaries, pastors or evangelists. We need to be devoted to living for Jesus, whatever we do, however we serve or support. We should also remember that the Christian life of 'doing' stems from relationship – 'being' with God. We know and love God. Our 'works' will stem from that. As we grow ever closer to him, his Spirit flows out to the people he places in our path.

Let's pray for Paul's passion in living devoted lives for God. If we are leaders, let's ensure 'our people' can trust us to be as faithful and dependable as Titus – strong in the truth, refuting lies and error, and always loving the God of mercy and grace.

Father, I want to be fully devoted to you. Help me to live the rest of my life loving you, spending time with you, serving you and blessing you. Amen.

SHEILA JACOBS

Water and springs in the Bible

Lakshmi Jeffreys writes:

As I prepared, prayed through and read around these studies on water and springs in the Bible, I wondered which passages you might choose. The Bible is full of stories involving water: creation; Noah and the flood; Moses leading God's people through the Red Sea into the wilderness where they became thirsty and fractious; Elijah's battle with the prophets of Baal during an extensive drought; Jesus walking on the lake; the disciples fishing – too many tales to recount in a short series of studies. In addition, water is often used as a metaphor for life or even death. Your choice of stories and ideas might be different from those you will encounter over the next two weeks. Please feel free to enjoy your own exploration of the theme as well as mine!

Perhaps our thoughts and feelings about water are influenced by our experience. As I type, I have just enjoyed a cup of tea and I am relieved my feet are drying following a muddy walk in the rain wearing leaky boots! I have been remembering our summer holiday by a lake, where we swam and played, and it is easy to recall my immense gratitude for a drink of water during a walk around the lake on a sunny afternoon. At the same time, while digesting news stories about floods, I am contemplating correspondence from a Christian charity, urging me to contribute to a project to bring water to a drought-ridden area of the world.

Water is essential for life. Jesus referred to himself as the source of living water, picking up on words of prophets centuries before. With this in mind, my aim in these studies is to focus not on water itself but on what the Bible says using the theme of water about God, the church, individual Christians or other people.

Finally, an image from Psalm 85:11–12: 'Faithfulness will spring up from the ground, and righteousness will look down from the sky. The Lord will give what is good' (NRSV). The picture that comes to mind is of springs of water from below and rain from above meeting to offer relief from dryness and despair, providing life and hope. Over the next two weeks, during the northern hemisphere's summer, may the Lord refresh you and restore you.

God's provision and purpose

Springs came up from the ground and watered all the land. (v. 6, NLT)

I love the creation stories of Genesis. The sense of delight, perhaps even playfulness, as God brings into being all life. Here, before there is anything or anyone, God has made provision. There is no rain, but water comes from the earth to prepare for the existence of both humans and others. God then places the man he has made in the garden of Eden. Everything is as it should be.

Springs from the earth and four rivers flowing from a garden are found in other ancient stories of creation. In many of these cultures, water was vital in a way that people living in northern Europe cannot fully grasp. The difference in the Genesis creation story is God's sovereignty. God is creating, preparing and permitting all life to flourish. God has a plan and has created humans to be involved with God's creation. Even when everything goes wrong, God continues to provide for the people and world he has created and loved. There is no blueprint, only relationship. God remains in charge, regardless of what happens.

Everyone subscribes to an idea of how the world came into being. Some of these are based on ancient myths, others on scientific discoveries. Perhaps Christians would do well to focus not on 'how' but 'why' God created the world. Concentrating on God's purpose and provision allows us to respond with thankfulness. As we remember Jesus' death and resurrection, we can be reassured of God's love and acceptance. We can return to God and discover our part in God's world.

Yesterday I saw a couple of goldfinches playing and gave thanks. Shortly afterwards, after hearing news of another human atrocity, I poured out my heart, praying for God to be seen to be sovereign in the midst of such terrible events. I don't need to understand God's plan; I simply need to speak and listen to him.

'The purpose of my instruction is that all believers would be filled with love that comes from a pure heart, a clear conscience, and genuine faith' (1 Timothy 1:4–5).

LAKSHMI JEFFREYS

Judgement and mercy

'Yes, I am confirming my covenant with you. Never again will floodwaters kill all living creatures; never again will a flood destroy the earth'. (v. 11, NLT)

God transformed water that brought life into water that brought death. Humanity had continued to ignore God. Noah was the only righteous individual. You know the story of the ark.

The flood arose because God hates sin. At the same time, God loves his creation and offered a fresh start. Raindrops act as prisms and the constituent colours of light shining through them result in a rainbow. God's picture of restored relationship appears literally through rain, the vehicle of judgement. What a beautiful metaphor of God's mercy and forgiveness!

Across the world, rainbows are symbols of hope, peace and solidarity. The late Archbishop Desmond Tutu described South Africa as a 'rainbow nation' following the first elections after apartheid. During the Covid pandemic in the UK, people placed rainbows in their windows to demonstrate support for the NHS. This use of rainbow imagery is powerful and brings people together. At the same time, the Christian view of rainbows goes beyond popular symbolism. Just as the account of the flood in Genesis is richer than that in other ancient literature, so for Christians, the rainbow is a sign of God's promise of hope until the final judgement. While there is always mercy, it is against the backdrop of judgement for sin. Relationship with God begins with returning to God – repentance.

God has promised never again to destroy the whole earth by flooding. Humanity has a responsibility to care for the planet and not exacerbate the likelihood of flooding. Every time I see a rainbow, I give thanks that God remains in control – of the weather, of all life. This spurs me into action and prayer when I hear about floods – whether local, where the church is able to offer practical support, or across the world, where we can give money and goods to relief agencies.

What are your thoughts and feelings about rainbows? How might God's mercy against the backdrop of judgement inform your prayer and action?

LAKSHMI JEFFREYS

God remains God

'Who closed the gates to hold back the sea when it burst from the womb of the earth?' (v. 8, GNT)

Flooding was about the only catastrophe not to afflict Job and his family! While many people find the story of Job depressing, it provides a vivid, accurate account of how different people respond to their own misfortune and that of others. I wince whenever I read the statements of blame made by Job's comforters, especially when Job refuses to accept their viewpoints of the nature of God and Job's sinfulness. Enter God to explain all!

Notice God does not justify or in any way explain what has happened to Job. Instead, God reminds Job and the others that God is God and they are not. Reminiscent of our first reading from Genesis, God's question to Job uses the image of water in creation. Almost midwife-like, God brings the sea to birth safely. Neither Job nor his companions can manage this!

The question of why 'bad things' happen to 'good people' has always vexed society. Job has an approach which bears consideration: he first examines himself to ensure he has not committed any sins (chapter 31). (He also makes sacrifices for sins his children might have committed unknowingly – chapter 1.) When dreadful things happen to him, he does not blame God but instead tells God and those around him how he feels. In turn, God responds, but not as anyone might expect.

It is unfair that the friend of a friend should have struggled to conceive, and then the long-awaited baby be born with significant additional needs. I can't begin to understand why a loving mother should have died in a freak accident, leaving her own widowed mother to manage both the loss of her daughter and the need to face terminal cancer without any immediate family support. As I come before God, I trust he will make himself known.

Hold before God anyone you know in significant distress – and ask for God's wisdom as you seek to listen to and support them.

LAKSHMI JEFFREYS

Rebellion

Tormented by thirst, they continued to argue with Moses. 'Why did you bring us out of Egypt? Are you trying to kill us, our children, and our livestock with thirst?' (v. 3, NLT)

Several years ago, a friend and I were travelling home in her car. The journey took nearly three hours, and for at least two and a half of these, her two-year-old daughter was distraught in the back. Nothing we did could pacify the child – snacks, games, cuddles were all to no avail. That evening my friend phoned and told me the reason for the distress – you guessed it, the little girl was thirsty! I am reliably informed that humans can survive for two or three days without water, but for this child – and for the hapless adults with her – two hours produced torment. Multiply this distress by a few thousand and you can understand Moses' concern for his life when the people were arguing with him in the desert. Meribah (argument) is an apt nickname for this place.

How quickly the people forgot the miracles God had performed and the promised land they would inhabit. Enormous spiritual discipline is required to overcome immediate physical needs, as Jesus demonstrated when tempted by the devil in the wilderness. God always keeps his promises, and there is never any need to test God (as Jesus reminded the devil in the same setting). Yet most of us, especially if our children were struggling, might find it hard to trust God.

Rebellion arises when people do not trust the leader to provide what everyone needs. Because Moses was the only one who had access to God, the people turned on him. Through Christ, we have the privilege of addressing God directly.

How can I learn to trust God when my immediate needs or those of people I love most appear to be overlooked?

LAKSHMI JEFFREYS

Metaphor for hope and life

Springs will gush forth in the wilderness, and streams will water the wasteland. The parched ground will become a pool, and springs of water will satisfy the thirsty land. Marsh grass and reeds and rushes will flourish where desert jackals once lived. (vv. 6–7, NLT)

Setting aside debate about the authorship and date of Isaiah, this passage is brimming with hope and joy for God's people. In ancient times, anyone who was ill or disabled was considered to be like a desert: barren, worthless and about to die. Yet here is a prophecy about how God will bring to life that which was thought to be without hope. The images are so powerful that no individual or group of people could possibly conjure such wonders. Only God can bring about such transformation, from death to life.

Hope is always rooted in God and joy is a by-product of God's presence. Yet society seems obsessed with how to be happy and fulfilled through an individual's own efforts. By following so many steps, anyone can overcome their unfortunate circumstances and become the person they want to be. It feels significant that the images of life in this passage are not for an individual but for the whole land and an entire people. Fulfilment stops being an individual quest and becomes a shared journey.

Metaphors for the church in the New Testament – household, living stones, body and so on – demonstrate how God works with the limitations of an individual to build a dynamic servant. Perhaps as we focus on Jesus' suffering, death and resurrection as the source of our hope, we shall be more alert to God's work in and through us within our communities. Contrary to what was expected at the time, women stayed with Jesus at the foot of the cross and a woman was the first to see the resurrected Jesus and to tell the good news to the scared disciples. How might God work through what you or society see as limitations?

Read slowly through the verses. Which metaphors jump out? Spend time praying about these.

LAKSHMI JEFFREYS

Rejecting pure water

They have forsaken me, the fountain of living water, and dug out cisterns for themselves, cracked cisterns that can hold no water. (v. 13, NRSV)

Sewing is not one of my gifts. I recall with embarrassment the needlework lesson at school, during which my teacher genuinely could not work out which way up to hold the garment I had attempted to create. So why, years later, did I insist on making curtains for the bay window in our sitting room? In the end, I constructed one and a friend who was a gifted seamstress made the other. It was not difficult to tell the difference between the two and unsurprising that mine was soon 'remedied'. Even worse, someone had previously offered to make the curtains for me, but I was stubborn and had to do things my way, even if the result was pitiful.

God's people took this trait further. God's lament in our passage is heartbreaking. He had rescued them from Egypt and given them the perfect land. He defended them from enemies and offered the means to live fully and well. Instead, the people turned away from God to the worthless, impotent idols worshipped by the surrounding nations. The privilege of travelling in parts of South Asia and East Africa, where running water can be a luxury, brings home the power of the prophet's words and the insanity of the people. They rejected the source of life in order to feel autonomous. Sin – choosing my own way and ignoring God – has 'I' in the middle. Replace God with the desire to do what I want, my way, and disaster strikes.

The effects of climate change, a direct result of human sin, are seen worldwide. Hotter summers in Europe lead to widespread droughts. Other parts of the world experience devastating flooding. Along with practical solutions and ideas to be more aware of the environment, perhaps we need to repent and return to the source of living water.

What idols have we chosen instead of God to result in climate challenges? Pray for all who work for healing and hope in this area.

LAKSHMI JEFFREYS

God's gift of life

There will be swarms of living things wherever the water of this river flows. Fish will abound in the Dead Sea, for its waters will become fresh. Life will flourish wherever this water flows. (v. 9, NLT)

The lowest point on earth, the Dead Sea, is a lake. Although it is fed by the River Jordan, it has five times more salt than any ocean and hardly any rainfall. As a result, only a few bacteria and other microorganisms can survive there. Perhaps you have 'floated' in or seen pictures of people lying in the Dead Sea. These geographical facts make Ezekiel's prophecy almost too miraculous to comprehend. To increase amazement, these words were written to God's people in exile, the result of rejecting God's living water (see yesterday). Having seen the temple in Jerusalem destroyed, God's people were given a picture of a new temple from which a life-giving river would flow. Not only would the water sustain life in the surrounding trees (all fresh water would do this), but it would also bring life to areas which had only ever known death. God was offering restoration and fresh hope; life out of death; God's presence in and through worship.

All of these promises were fulfilled in the life, death and resurrection of Jesus. Enabled by the Holy Spirit, through prayer, the Bible and the church, we can experience and share God's gifts of hope and life. These Christian truths are so familiar that we might sometimes take them for granted. When was the last time you really thought about the power and love of God transforming salt water into fresh water? If that impossible picture can be realised, perhaps it is worth praying for God to transform stagnant relationships, to soften the areas of my heart that have been hardened over the years and to rejuvenate tired worship among God's people.

Gaze on the temple as Ezekiel describes it. Marvel at the river flowing from it. Pray for life in the dead areas God reveals to you.

LAKSHMI JEFFREYS

The first miracle

What Jesus did here in Cana of Galilee was the first of the signs through which he revealed his glory; and his disciples believed in him. (v. 11, NIV)

One of the many privileges of my job is conducting weddings. Couples are often shocked when I tell them I hope their wedding day will not be the happiest of their life – instead, may it be the happiest of their life to date. The wedding is intended to be a celebration of and prelude to a lifelong, lifegiving marriage. As husband and wife look back at the day, I pray they will remember the presence of family, friends and God as they embarked on their journey as Mr and Mrs – maybe especially important when the marriage goes through a challenging phase.

John's gospel does not speak of miracles but signs – signposts to God's rule. In heaven, there will be a banquet; on earth, a crisis at a wedding is miraculously overcome when Jesus turns ordinary water into the very best wine. In heaven, every knee will bow before Jesus; on earth, only Jesus' mother and a handful of servants know the author of the transformation, but everyone at the wedding benefits.

The conversion of water into wine occurs after Mary, Jesus' mother, tells the servants to do whatever Jesus tells them. The only other occasion we encounter Mary in John's gospel is at the foot of the cross. It is sobering to consider that Mary next views water and blood (symbolised these days by wine in a Communion service) after her son's death. Although all of us know, we need to be reminded that God works on God's terms, and we need to listen and obey. What follows will be more remarkable than we could possibly imagine. It is not an accident that the miracle in Cana takes place on the third day.

Pray for married couples to be open and obedient to the transforming power of God's love.

LAKSHMI JEFFREYS

Miracles and faith

Jesus came towards them, walking on the water. When the disciples saw him walking on the water, they were terrified. In their fear, they cried out... (vv. 25-26, NLT)

Yesterday we saw the transformation of water into wine, as people obeyed Jesus. Today's miracle involving water could not be more different. The disciples have had a day of miracles. Jesus has just fed 5,000 people using a packed lunch of bread and fish. He has gone off to pray as the disciples make their way in a boat across the lake. During a horrific storm, they see a ghostly figure approach on the water!

With the benefit of the whole gospel, it is easy to marvel at the disciples' lack of faith. After all, they had seen within the past few hours that Jesus had power and authority beyond their wildest dreams. Okay, it was dark and the middle of the night, when no one is at their best and there was a scary storm. But these people were experienced fishermen. They knew Jesus. Why didn't they recognise him? Why were they so scared?

News on social or other media is largely filled with fear and despair. While there might be a new cancer treatment, more people are ill with or dying of hundreds of cancers and other diseases. Society appears to promote doing everything for yourself, or possibly your family (at least those you get on with), rather than serving others. Living out Christian faith, sharing God's hope, healing, love and transformation is not easy. Christians are constantly battling the elements – it is hard to recognise Jesus in the midst of the storms we face. Even when we try to follow, like Peter, as soon as we take our eyes off the one who calls us, we sink. Praise God that he continues to work in, through and around us, regardless of how little faith we might have!

Loving God, forgive my lack of faith. Help me to fix my eyes on you and to heed your call, even if circumstances seem impossible. Amen.

LAKSHMI JEFFREYS

The water of life

'Those who drink of the water that I will give them will never be thirsty. The water that I will give will become in them a spring of water gushing up to eternal life.' (v. 14, NRSV)

The story of Jesus' conversation with the Samaritan woman and all that resulted is worth reading slowly and prayerfully. You might imagine the heat of the midday sun, the loneliness of the setting (all the 'acceptable' women are in their homes), and the need for the woman to draw water for drinking and washing despite her desire not to encounter anyone from the village. And here, at the well, is a man. She knows all about men. But this one is different. To begin with, he is the enemy. In addition, these men rarely speak to their own women in public, let alone a foreigner. Yet he asks her for a drink.

'Living' water is what we might term flowing water, in a stream or river, rather than that in a canal, for example. Of course, Jesus speaks of more than water in which fish and other life flourishes: he has come to bring life itself in all its fullness (John 10:10). Later, Jesus speaks of the Holy Spirit and streams of living water (John 7:37–39). No wonder the woman wants the drink Jesus offers. At the same time, Jesus leaves her in no doubt that accepting his gift of life will change everything – her ideas, her actions and her relationships. She attempts to deflect the conversation, but Jesus knows all about her. Bemused and exhilarated, the woman eventually invites everyone in town to meet Jesus and experience salvation for themselves.

Jesus' offer of living water remains available to all of us. If we accept, we too will have our ideas, actions and relationships transformed. This process is not always comfortable, and, like the woman, it can be tempting to distract Jesus from identifying the area of life which needs to be washed clean.

Read the story again, and ask Jesus to show you if there is an area of your life requiring transformation. Then rejoice with your friends and neighbours and invite them to meet him too!

LAKSHMI JEFFREYS

Integrity

Can both fresh water and salt water flow from the same spring? (v. 11, NIV)

As someone who preaches and teaches for a living, I find this passage at best challenging and at worst convicting! Even if we are not addressing large groups of people, our words matter. How many times have you been wounded by a careless comment or unkind criticism? How often has something come out of your mouth that you have immediately regretted and wanted to retract? When our son was younger, he would hear us speaking and ask if we would make the same statement if the individual was in the room. It was a salutary lesson.

While James is speaking about the tongue and spoken words, the same applies to anything published on social media. The results of thoughtlessness or malice can be catastrophic and, on the internet, can be both reported worldwide and remain forever. It does not take long to research a celebrity and find something they said or wrote perhaps hastily and certainly not considering the consequences. We need to heed James' warning.

Fresh water and salt water cannot flow from the same spring. Over time, what we say and write betrays what we believe. If we truly accept that each human being is created in the image of God, then whatever we think of their actions, it is God's role to judge, not ours. Jesus reminded people that what comes out of our mouths betrays what is in our hearts (Luke 6:45). Try as we might, it is impossible to control our words unless we are rooted in Christ and washed clean by the Holy Spirit.

A godly mother and grandmother constantly reminded her family and anyone in her home: 'If it isn't kind or isn't true, don't say it.'

Spend time reflecting on recent conversations. If you have said anything unkind or untrue, confess this to God. Ask the Spirit of truth to guide you into all truth.

LAKSHMI JEFFREYS

True or false?

These people are springs without water and mists driven by a storm. (v. 17a, NIV)

Waterless springs promise much and deliver nothing. Mists driven by a storm might soak you as you walk through them, but they will not water the parched ground below. False teaching might have a semblance of truth but does not encourage hearers to pursue Christian discipleship. Peter has no time for anyone who suggests that Jesus is simply one of many good teachers or a prophet who promotes a lifestyle incompatible with love, joy, peace and other fruit of the Spirit. He does not hold back in his condemnation, as he reminds those he is addressing of the fate of equivalent characters in the Old Testament. (If you have time, you might want to discover what happened to Lot, to Sodom and Gomorrah or to Balaam and the donkey.)

Disciples of Jesus will make mistakes and sometimes sin deliberately. Yet, when confronted by the truth, they will confess their wrongdoing, repent and seek God's ways again. False teachers, on the other hand, invite people to follow rules or offer what appears to be freedom but soon becomes addiction because there are no limits offered. (Christians are indeed free to eat any food but we are not to damage ourselves, other people or God's world, with our food choices.)

Sue's granddaughtr was anxious as they drove past Sue's church. The little girl had heard both her grandmothers speak about being Christian and belonging to Jesus. Yet the child's other grandmother had said people who worshipped at Sue's church belonged to the devil. Sue gently suggested anyone who followed Jesus would show Jesus' characteristics of love, kindness and so on wherever they worshipped and wherever they were. A few months later, Sue's granddaughter asked to come to Sue's church. She wanted to live like Jesus, not join a sect.

Watch out for false prophets... By their fruit you will recognise them. (Matthew 7:15–16, NIV)

LAKSHMI JEFFREYS

A terrifying vision

The serpent poured water like a river after the woman, to sweep her away with the flood. (v. 15, NRSV)

Until Jesus comes again, the church will battle against false prophets, subtle deception, an increasingly hostile world and the temptation to compromise. This is the overall message of the second half of John's vision in Revelation. The stories of the woman and the dragon and of Michael battling Satan are vivid and unsettling.

In today's passage, the river is not the living water we find elsewhere but instead is employed by the enemy to destroy the woman who gave birth to the Saviour. At this, the earth swallows up the water, leaving an angry dragon, determined to wage war against other Christians.

Apocalyptic literature in the Bible, filled with dragons, visions, monsters and other images, is multilayered. John was in exile, writing to a persecuted church. Life was utterly grim, but the vision would have reminded the recipients that God would ultimately triumph. (Michael and the angels evicted the dragon and others from heaven.) The small band of Christians, desperate to hear from one of Jesus' closest friends, would be reassured to know their circumstances were both understood by God and predicted. They could stand firm in the knowledge that the church would not be destroyed. Thinking about parts of the world today, where being known to be a Christian will result in imprisonment or even death, the message remains agonisingly relevant. Whatever our circumstances or situation, all Christians are called to fight against evil.

The Bible reminds us that we battle not against flesh and blood but principalities and powers. Praise God that we are on the winning side, and pray for anyone who might doubt this.

LAKSHMI JEFFREYS

A beautiful vision

Then the angel showed me the river of the water of life, bright as crystal, flowing from the throne of God and of the Lamb through the middle of the street of the city. (vv. 1–2, NRSV)

After yesterday's drama, today's picture is a profound and exquisite relief. Unlike the vision offered by Ezekiel (last Saturday), the river in this vision is flowing through the city. There is no temple, because God is the temple. God, the Lamb that was slain, and people are alongside each other forever in worship. The presence of the river shows that the city is also a garden. Unlike the first garden, Eden, where Adam and Eve were told they could not eat the fruit of a certain tree, this final garden is different. The river in John's vision brings living water to the tree of life. Anyone can eat anything. Eternal life has no boundaries. However ghastly the circumstances of the persecuted Christians to whom John wrote, there was hope. Suffering would be transformed into life and love for everyone.

Our dog loves water and, as long as she knows she can get out, will enter any stream, canal, river or even the sea to swim, play and be refreshed. She would adore the clear fresh river depicted here. The lack of algae or anything harmful means she could plunge in and consume freely. Praying about this final reflection, I have been encouraged to immerse myself in Jesus – to be washed clean, to be invigorated and to drink deeply. I have become aware of my part in bringing life and hope to those around me from the water of life. The picture of heaven is more than an offer of hope after death; we might occasionally have a foretaste here on earth. So, I invite you to imitate our dog and leap into the living water as you pray. Allow the Holy Spirit to cleanse and revive you to experience God's hope and peace today.

'Jesus gives us life if we drink the living water, sing it so that everybody knows' (from the song 'Have you heard the raindrops drumming on roof-tops?' by Christian Strover).

LAKSHMI JEFFREYS

Friends with God, friends with others

Amy Boucher Pye writes:

We've moved from the coronavirus pandemic to one of friendlessness. According to my friend Sheridan Voysey, founder of the Friendship Lab, those without close friends are on the rise – around a quarter of people in the UK, US and Australia have no close friends, including one in ten who have no friends at all. And, he observes, most people struggle to make or maintain friendships after the age of 35, mainly because of being busy with work and family demands, along with individualism.

I find these statistics heartbreaking – the thought of so many people without dear friends – and I wonder where you fall within them. If you long for friends, as I did when I first moved to the UK, I'm breathing a prayer that God would answer that desire. Please, Lord.

God has made us for himself and for each other. He longs for us to have strong friendships not only with himself, but also with our neighbours and family. With the help of the Holy Spirit dwelling within, we can find, make and keep friends. And God promises to strengthen his friendship with us.

Our fortnight on this topic therefore explores not only God's friendship with his people but also the person-to-person relationships detailed in his word. We find encouragement and instruction – examples of what not to do as much as how to be a friend. We'll move through the scriptures from Genesis to Revelation as we explore, ponder and pray.

I hope that these weeks we travel together will spur you on in love. As we begin, I invite you to spend some time in prayer – perhaps you could go on a walk with Jesus, if possible. As you stroll together in the city or the countryside, enjoy the time together. You might ask him to bring to mind the image of someone – perhaps a long-time friend, a new acquaintance or a colleague. Commit to praying for that person as we move through the fortnight. Maybe God will spur you on to serve them in some way as well!

I count so many readers as friends now, having written these notes for so many years. I close with gratitude as I picture many of you, giving thanks for your words of encouragement, your questions, and yes, your words of correction. May you experience showers of grace, joy and love from the one who wants to be your closest Friend.

Unashamed

**The man said, 'This is now bone of my bones and flesh of my flesh'…
Adam and his wife were both naked, and they felt no shame. (v. 23 and
v. 25, NIV)**

Our starting point with friendship in the Bible falls right at the very beginning of the story of God and his people. Why? Because God wove in this
theme right from the start. After he created Adam and found 'no suitable
helper' for him (v. 20), he created Eve, making them not only for each other,
but also them for him. He wanted them to build a beautiful community
where people lived with each other, and with God, with pure transparency:
'Adam and his wife were both naked, and they felt no shame' (v. 25).

Yet we know the story all too well. Eve and Adam ate the forbidden fruit
and shame came shooting into the garden. No longer could they look at
God without feeling disgraced and sorry for what they'd done, blaming
each other and Satan. Their friendship with each other and with God was
marred irrevocably.

We may rue the opening story of the Bible, longing for life in the garden
when friends don't betray us, when we can trust that a loved one will never
disappoint us. Those days are long gone, but God has put in a rescue plan.
When we're fully in his presence in heaven, we'll no longer be under the
curse (see Revelation 22:3) and we'll enjoy pure friendships with each other
and with God. In the meantime, we can lean on the Holy Spirit to help us
love each other.

I invite you to spend some time considering, with your imagination,
what life in God's garden was like before sin entered the world. Picture
yourself naked and unashamed, communing with your Maker and your
loved ones. How might God speak to you as you place yourself in those
surroundings?

---

*Loving creator God, I'm sorry for the things I do – and the things I leave
undone – that bring me shame. Through your Holy Spirit, help me to show
and receive love in ways that honour you. Amen.*

AMY BOUCHER PYE

Belief

You see that his faith and his actions were working together, and his faith was made complete by what he did. And the scripture was fulfilled that says, 'Abraham believed God, and it was credited to him as righteousness,' and he was called God's friend. (vv. 22–23, NIV)

God promised Abraham that he would make him the father of nations; the childless man had only to obey and believe. But over the following decades, when his wife Sarah remained barren, Abraham wavered in his belief. For instance, he passed off Sarah as his sister when they travelled through Egypt, and only God sending diseases on Pharoah and his house-hold saved her honour (see Genesis 12:10–20). Later he agreed to sleep with his servant girl, Hagar, so she would bear him his heir (see Genesis 16). He wasn't trusting God and his promises.

If God can call such a man with these failings his friend, there's hope for us all! That's what James wrote in his letter to what he names as the twelve tribes scattered around. He points out that it's Abraham's belief that credits him with righteousness. God is not ashamed to call him his friend.

We only need to believe! We might have failed God and others, but he promises to forgive us when we come to him and repent of our wrong-doing. We might think that God is silent and that he won't deliver on his promises, but we can ask him to give us more faith to continue to believe. Abraham and Sarah needed to do this at times over the years – after all, they finally became parents at the ages of 100 and 90! They may have wavered in their beliefs, but they never gave up.

Ponder which of God's promises you hold on to firmly and which you're tempted to discount or dismiss. Why? How can you look to God for help to believe?

God the Father of all, thank you for extending friendship to Abraham, even though he failed you. Help me to trust you and to believe in you, now and tomorrow. Amen.

AMY BOUCHER PYE

Face to face

Whenever the people saw the pillar of cloud standing at the entrance to the tent, they all stood and worshipped, each at the entrance to their tent. The Lord would speak to Moses face to face, as one speaks to a friend. (vv. 10–11, NIV)

Have you ever considered how truly amazing it is that we live after Pentecost, meaning that if we believe in Jesus we are filled with his Holy Spirit? As I read through passages in the Old Testament – which I love doing – I burst with gratitude that God has made his Spirit available to us all. After all, before the coming of the Spirit after Jesus' death and resurrection, the Spirit only settled on certain people, often prophets and God's leaders.

Moses would reflect God's glory visibly; when he'd come down from the mountain where he met with God, his face would shine and glow. So much so that he covered his face with a veil so that the people wouldn't fear him (see Exodus 34:29–35). Another sign of God's presence was the pillar of cloud that would stand at the entrance to the tent of meeting. Ponder this lovely line and what it confers: 'The Lord would speak to Moses face to face, as one speaks to a friend' (Exodus 33:11).

Because of his sins, when out of frustration with God's people Moses didn't follow God's instructions fully, Moses didn't get to enter the promised land. Although he didn't enter the land of milk and honey, he remained God's friend, with God burying him in sight of the promised land. And Moses was able to commission and mentor Joshua, who then led God's people out of the desert and into the land where God wanted them to thrive.

So too for us. As we saw with Abraham and now with Moses, God doesn't give up on his people. Nor will he abandon them. He's the Friend who will never let us down, never betray us, never turn his face from us.

Consider and receive God's promise to Moses: 'My Presence will go with you, and I will give you rest' (Exodus 33:14).

AMY BOUCHER PYE

True kindness

'Don't urge me to leave you or to turn back from you. Where you go I will go, and where you stay I will stay. Your people will be my people and your God my God. Where you die I will die, and there I will be buried.' (vv. 16–17, NIV)

God's intent for friendship is that it is multigenerational, which we see reflected in the lovely relationship between Ruth and Naomi. As I consider their friendship, I think of the women a decade or two ahead of me who have befriended me over the years and given me so much wisdom, love, affirmation and care. A few have now died, and although I miss them, I think of them revelling in God's presence, no longer afflicted with money woes or with a voice made husky from working in a smoky restaurant. I consider too of how I want to pray for more friends a couple of decades younger than I am, as I am sadly lacking in that way! What a privilege it would be to shower someone younger with love, even as I have received.

After the death of her menfolk, Naomi is bereft. Urging her daughters-in-law to go back home, she expects to be alone. But Ruth won't leave her. Instead, she vows to become a foreigner – to take on Naomi's people as her people and Naomi's God as her God. That's how committed she is to the older woman – even unto death.

God honoured Ruth's steadfast devotion and saved Ruth and Naomi from starvation. He even found Ruth a new husband who would care for and love these widows. And through it all, they had their friendship with each other to keep each other strong.

Why not, today, make a list of your friends. If you feel lacking, ask God to help you reach out to someone and befriend them. Perhaps he might bring you some friends to affirm and to mentor!

God who cares for the widows and the bereft, thank you for wonderful friends who uphold me and encourage me. Help me to be a loving friend today. Amen.

AMY BOUCHER PYE

One in spirit

And Jonathan made a covenant with David because he loved him as himself. Jonathan took off the robe he was wearing and gave it to David, along with his tunic, and even his sword, his bow and his belt.
(vv. 3–4, NIV)

They were unlikely friends – one a prince, in line to become king, the other a poor shepherd boy. But Jonathan and David became the best of friends, so close that they were 'one in spirit' (v. 1). They supported each other through the ups and downs of life with King Saul, Jonathan's father, such as probably meeting at the palace when David played the harp to soothe the king's nerves or when David had to escape from the king who wanted to eliminate him.

Jonathan could have been jealous of this younger friend, but he supported him through it all – he even gave David his tunic and his armour, signifying that he was making the way for David to be anointed king instead of him. In a sacrificial way, Jonathan 'loved him as himself', and in doing so followed the great commandment to love one's neighbour as oneself (Leviticus 19:18).

With this story God confirms the value of friends. They aren't compelled to love each other – they haven't made the vows of husband and wife, for instance – nor are they family, with those ties that bind. But the bond between these friends can be so strong that one puts the other's needs before their own.

As I think of the gifts I receive from friends, I give thanks – for those who read my writing and give me feedback; for those who make me meals and give me a bed when travelling; for those who entrust me with their private pains, that I might support them and pray. What about you? Which friends have loved you sacrificially, and when have you put someone's needs before your own? Ask God to help you to remember acts of kindness and giving, that you might thank him – and perhaps thank your friend too.

Loving God, continue to fill me with your Spirit, that I might show love to my friends and to those in need. Give me your eyes to see these people as those beloved by you, made in your image. Amen.

AMY BOUCHER PYE

True commitment

Elijah said to Elisha, 'Stay here; the Lord has sent me to Bethel.' But Elisha said, 'As surely as the Lord lives and as you live, I will not leave you.' (v. 2, NIV)

Dogged determination – I like that in a friend. I think of Klara, one committed to work through the hard things instead of bailing. When I chose to support another friend over her, she was hurt but didn't abandon our friendship. We had to endure some tough conversations but eventually came through stronger for them.

I like the dogged determination of both Elijah and Elisha in this story from 2 Kings. They and the other prophets all seem to know that Elijah will be taken to heaven that day – perhaps they'd had a prophecy from God. Again and again Elisha's commitment to stay with Elijah is tested, not only from the man himself, but from those around them. 'Yes,' says Elisha, 'I know you're going, but I won't leave you.' And to the company of prophets, he says, 'Be quiet!' Perhaps he's dreading losing his friend and mentor, and he doesn't want to hear the chatter of the prophets around him.

We might wonder if Elisha is being greedy when he asks Elijah for a double portion of his spirit (v. 9), but this request was rooted in the cultural practices for the inheritance of the firstborn (see Deuteronomy 21:17). Note Elijah's dependence on God when he replies that he doesn't know if this request will be fulfilled (v. 10). He puts it before God, but can't make any promises if God will deliver.

Of course, the one with the most tenacious commitment to his people is God. Although his people fail him time and time again, he never throws in the towel and calls it quits. He came through to Elisha, as the prophet saw Elijah swept into heaven, and he comes through for us. He is unwavering in his love for you and for me.

Loving God, you will never give up on me. Help me to be like Elisha, one who stays with their friends to the end. I want to share your love and care. Amen.

AMY BOUCHER PYE

Living united

How good and pleasant it is when God's people live together in unity! It is like precious oil poured on the head, running down on the beard, running down on Aaron's beard, down on the collar of his robe. (vv. 1–2, NIV)

For seven years I lived with three other women outside of Washington, DC, sharing a home and our lives together. We had various different groupings of housemates over the years, but one other woman and I remained the anchors in the home. She and I loved each other, but we could also drive each other crazy at times – so different were we! Once, when putting together a rota for divvying up the various cleaning jobs, I placed this verse at the bottom of the sheet, personalising it: 'How good and pleasant it is when sisters live together in unity!' v. 1). The visual reminder on the fridge helped us to love each other, even when we had to ask God for an extra dollop of grace.

King David penned this psalm to praise God for the gift of unity. He pictured it as a precious oil running down someone's head, which would fit the ancient Near Eastern practice of anointing a visitor to welcome and refresh them. The scent of the oil would bring them all joy during their visit and afterwards. David also likened this unity between God's people as the dew from the mountains – clear, refreshing and a blessing of the Lord.

If we have lived in a home of strife, we can nod in agreement with David at these visual reminders of the gift of unity between friends and family. If you are in conflict with someone just now, might you spend time today asking God how he could smooth the relationship with his oils and living water? If you have no angst among your people, why not pray for some of them individually, asking God to bless them.

God of all unity, I ask you for your love and grace, that I might love those who grate on me. Help me to extend to them mercy, kindness and peace. Amen.

AMY BOUCHER PYE

A scorching fire

A perverse person stirs up conflict, and a gossip separates close friends. A violent person entices their neighbour and leads them down a path that is not good. (vv. 28–29, NIV)

'They said *what*?' I exclaimed. The news of the untrue words that were whispered about me felt like a physical blow – a punch to the stomach that limited the air I could inhale. My immediate reaction was to defend myself, and I started to put together the bullet points in my mind. But later, after a conversation with my husband, I realised that in this instance the best way forward was to say nothing.

In the Bible, God gives us examples of wonderful friendships, but he also highlights the damage done when friends betray us and cause us pain. Solomon, sharing his wisdom in Proverbs, shares the damage that a loose tongue can inflict: 'A scoundrel plots evil, and on their lips it is like a scorching fire' (v. 27). Note how visual the second half of that verse is, bringing forth the image of a fire that builds and spreads. These flames can destroy friendships too: 'A gossip separates close friends' (v. 28).

Some friendships can never be restored, like the one I alluded to above. Without clear reconciliation, I couldn't trust that former friend, and although it pained me to lose her as a confidante and prayer partner, I understood that our formerly close friendship was over. But other times we can repair the gash, especially when we follow Solomon's wisdom: 'Gracious words are a honeycomb, sweet to the soul and healing to the bones' (v. 24).

If you've suffered gossip, why not ask God if you have any remaining shards of broken glass embedded in your heart that you need him to remove? If not, you could pray for those who have, that God would bring healing, hope and restoration.

God of grace and mercy, forgive me when I've been the one to spread false-hoods about someone else. Help me to repent and do what is right to make amends. Lead me to speak gracious words, for your glory. Amen.

AMY BOUCHER PYE

Threefold cord

Two are better than one, because they have a good return for their labour: if either of them falls down, one can help the other up. But pity anyone who falls and has no one to help them up. (vv. 9–10, NIV)

When I think about this passage from Ecclesiastes, I often link it to wedding services – it beautifully describes the desire of the couple to love each other, with the help of God. But I also think of it when remembering my childhood neighbourhood. Those on our street formed strong bonds through the challenges and joys of life, such as when my little brother spent weeks in the hospital when he was just three years old. Our neighbours helped our family with practical and emotional support. Our ties were deepened, and the fact that we shared faith in God – expressed through different denominations – tightened the links all the more.

Our neighbours were there to help us up when we fell (v. 10); they shared in our labour, making it easier and more productive (v. 9). With them standing with us, we didn't feel overpowered by the challenges that faced us (v. 12). I rather took the gift of them for granted as I grew up, knowing no other reality, but now, these decades later, I breathe my gratitude to God for this strand of many threads.

King Solomon probably wrote these words at the end of his life as he looked back over his follies and foibles. The beauty of this passage from chapter 4 stands in contrast to much of the rest of the book, where he shares the meaninglessness of life without God. Yet at the end he calls the reader back to their Creator as he concludes: 'Fear God and keep his commandments, for this is the duty of all mankind' (12:13).

We too can ask God to strengthen our faith in him, that our lives would have meaning and hope through his presence and that our relationships would be like a threefold cord, with him at the heart.

God of the neighbourhood, give me love for those who live around me, whether I know them or not. Help me to serve them joyfully, spreading your love and perhaps even sparking in them a curiosity about you. Amen.
AMY BOUCHER PYE

Anointing Jesus

Here a dinner was given in Jesus' honour. Martha served, while Lazarus was among those reclining at the table with him. Then Mary took about half a litre of pure nard, an expensive perfume; she poured it on Jesus' feet and wiped his feet with her hair. (vv. 2–3, NIV)

Some of Jesus' closest friends, outside of his disciples, were the trio of siblings from Bethany: Mary, Martha and Lazarus. John even says that Jesus loved them: 'Now Jesus loved Martha and her sister and Lazarus' (John 11:5). And yet he allowed Lazarus to die, delaying his arrival to the sisters until after they knew he was well and truly dead. The sisters, if they could have time-travelled to join Teresa of Ávila, might have echoed her admonishment to God: 'If this is how you treat your friends, no wonder you have so few of them!'

But as we read on in John 11, Jesus raised Lazarus from the dead to bring glory to God and to show that he, Jesus, is the resurrection and the life. We join the siblings in the next chapter, with each of them showing their love and friendship to Jesus in their individual ways – Martha serves Jesus, Lazarus reclines with him and Mary pours out precious oil to anoint him as she prepares for his death.

Her act of love isn't received wholeheartedly by those in her presence – Judas objects vociferously, for his own twisted motives, and Mark's gospel reports Jesus' disciples agreeing with him. As with Mary, we too will receive criticism at times when we pour out our love on our friends. We can do so unselfconsciously, knowing that God receives them with joy and will defend us, even as Jesus spoke out in support of Mary.

You might want to spend some time in prayer, asking God to help you discern how you might pour out your precious oil on him or on your friends. Trust that he will lead and guide you and that he welcomes your desire to give him honour through your act.

Loving Jesus, you receive my love and adoration. Thank you for dying and rising again, for showering me with your affection. I receive it and want to share it with others today. Amen.

AMY BOUCHER PYE

Friends, not servants

You are my friends if you do what I command. I no longer call you servants, because a servant does not know his master's business. Instead, I have called you friends, for everything that I learned from my Father I have made known to you. (vv. 14–15, NIV)

We might feel a pang of envy for the disciples and how they got to know Jesus in the flesh, eating with him and receiving from him. But as we read in John's gospel, during Jesus' last discussion with his friends before he's betrayed by Judas in the garden of Gethsemane, he will share the Spirit with us and make his knowledge of his Father known to his friends.

In this passage on love, Jesus calls his disciples his friends – and therefore, by extension, he names us as his friends. We remain in the love of God when we obey Jesus, just as he remains in the love of the Father because he keeps the Father's commands. Obedience here is key, and we might too easily pass by this word. But when we obey, we follow Jesus' joy in the Father by having joy in him. Wonderful, circular, pulsating love – amazing!

This love is not to hoard but to share: 'Love each other as I have loved you' (v. 12). Jesus welcomes us too, to know our master's business. He shares everything he's learned from his Father – *everything*! Have you ever considered that? There's no secret knowledge, no hidden agendas or special clubs for people in the know. What Jesus learns, he shares with us. And we collaborate with him to build his kingdom here on earth.

We therefore need not look at Jesus' friends with a pang of jealousy, for we too have the presence of Jesus with us. He calls us friend, and we can therefore love those around us – even the irritable, grumpy ones. We too will bear fruit that lasts, not sour or ill-formed pieces that stay bitter and never ripen.

'If you remain in me and I in you, you will bear much fruit; apart from me you can do nothing… This is to my Father's glory, that you bear much fruit, showing yourselves to be my disciples' (John 15:5, 8).

AMY BOUCHER PYE

Friends or enemies

You adulterous people, don't you know that friendship with the world means enmity against God? Therefore, anyone who chooses to be a friend of the world becomes an enemy of God. (v. 4, NIV)

God wants our whole self – all of our devotion, adoration and commitment. He brooks no rivals, and although sometimes we may feel uncomfortable by the uncompromising nature of certain passages in the Bible – such as this one in James – we can't ignore the admonition to give God all of who we are and all of who we will be. In writing to the Christians in the early church, James reminded them that their acrimony with each other was rooted in unrighteous desires. For true friendship with their neighbours, they would need to submit themselves fully to God, not seeking friendship with the world.

Note James' use of 'you adulterous people' (v. 4). Here he hearkens back to the Old Testament way of naming God's people as married to him. When they looked to those of the world to fill their deepest needs, they were idolatrous in God's sight. In short, when they were friends with the world, they were enemies of God (v. 4). And God was jealous (v. 5).

But all is not lost. God reaches out to the humble, showing them favour and giving them grace (v. 6). When we submit to him, humbling ourselves before him, he will lift us up (v. 10). We only need to pause, repent and lean on him.

If you have some time today, I invite you to read through this passage prayerfully four times, each time with a different emphasis of reading, reflecting, responding and resting. Ask God through his Spirit to highlight a word or phrase for you. Trust that he will speak to you, and ask for his discernment and wisdom in applying his truth to your life.

God, thank you that you feel jealous about what I desire. Help me not to look to the world for fulfilment but to you. You meet my deepest needs and aches; I seek your face this day. Amen.

AMY BOUCHER PYE

Spreading love

Above all, love each other deeply, because love covers over a multitude of sins. Offer hospitality to one another without grumbling. Each of you should use whatever gift you have received to serve others, as faithful stewards of God's grace in its various forms. (vv. 8–10, NIV)

When my husband and I had been married only a few months, we invited some lovely friends round to our flat for a meal. As Nicholas started to pour Steve a glass of water from a two-litre bottle, I shouted, 'No! That's the radiator water!' (By which I meant the water we kept to fill up the radiator on our ageing car.) Steve, never one to miss a quip, said, 'I have a verse for you… 1 Peter 4:9: "Practise hospitality"! I think you might need more practise at this!'

We all laughed, but I knew that I would need to learn how to love more deeply and to 'offer hospitality to one another without grumbling' (1 Peter 4:9), especially as I settled further into life in Britain. The lurking feeling that I was getting things wrong culturally made me less keen to put myself out there. But I also knew that God would give me strength to serve, for his glory and honour (v. 11). Interestingly, one Bible commentator notes that the term 'without grumbling' in Greek, the original language, involves a sense of muttering or speaking quietly as a way of expressing displeasure. That catches my eye, because I can think of more than once when I've uttered words under my breath in the kitchen. But Peter counsels those in the early church not to act in this way, instead loving each other deeply, 'because love covers over a multitude of sins' (v. 8).

Relationships can survive grumbles and disagreements when we spread a thick layer of love about. We might not feel like loving the one in our kitchen or our church sanctuary, but we can look to God and his grace to give us the will to serve. And he will answer.

God of all hospitality, you welcome me into your home. Help me in turn to welcome others into my home, that I might share your love and life. Amen.

AMY BOUCHER PYE

Welcoming Jesus

'Those whom I love I rebuke and discipline. So be earnest and repent. Here I am! I stand at the door and knock. If anyone hears my voice and opens the door, I will come in and eat with that person, and they with me'. (v. 19, NIV)

Many of us will be familiar with Holman Hunt's painting *The Light of the World*, which illustrates Revelation 3:20. Indeed, maybe we've visited the one displayed in St Paul's Cathedral. An often-noted detail about this picture is that the door handle hangs only on the inside – Jesus waits for us to open the door. He longs to be our friend, waiting for us to bid him inside to our homes and our hearts.

But what we often gloss over when we consider that painting is the context of the verse in this last chapter of the Bible. Note Jesus' words of admonition to those whom he loves – he will rebuke and discipline them. He will come in and eat with them, but his love will not leave them in a state of sin or wrongdoing.

Jesus convicts us of our shameful practices, our selfishness, the things we do that we shouldn't and those we don't do that we should. Why? Because he's a true friend. He speaks the hard words to us so that we can become more like him, with the help of the Holy Spirit dwelling within.

This is the discipline that the writer to the Hebrews speaks of, using the relationship of Father to children: 'God disciplines us for our good, in order that we may share in his holiness. No discipline seems pleasant at the time, but painful. Later on, however, it produces a harvest of righteousness and peace for those who have been trained by it' (Hebrews 12:10–11). If we feel that we're in this season of discipline, we can hold on to the promise of the harvest, and that Jesus will be with us in our home, eating at our table, when we but open the door to him.

Jesus, my friend, I welcome you to convict me of my wrongdoing, that I might become more like you. I long to produce a harvest of righteousness, in your time and by your means. Amen.

AMY BOUCHER PYE

Jonah: you can never outrun God's mercy

Claire Musters writes:

The story of Jonah is one that most of us will have been taught in Sunday school, but now we are adults, how well do we know it? With just 48 verses, it is one of the shortest books of the Bible – but do we know the full narrative? Children's versions of the story often focus on Jonah being swallowed by a big fish (or whale) and the fact that when he repents God allows him to be spat back on to shore. But this isn't quite the truth and actually misses out a whole chunk of the story, so in this study we are going to focus on a short set of verses each day to really dig into what is being said.

Jonah was a contemporary of two other biblical prophets, Amos and Joel. He was a prophet to Israel and Assyria, during the reign of Jeroboam II, who was king of Israel from 793–753 BC. He is mentioned in 2 Kings 14:25 and may have been part of the company of prophets that were mentioned in connection with Elisha's ministry – see 2 Kings 2:3. His words also reached the king of Judah in the southern kingdom – see 2 Kings 14:23–25.

So Jonah was a man of great standing in his community, and yet when God called him to take a message to Nineveh he ran in the opposite direction. Why? Some view this book of the Bible as a parable or other fictional tale, but there was a place called Nineveh and it was the most important city in Assyria (it became the capital 50 years later). However, its people were truly wicked. Any Israelite would have trembled at the idea of the Ninevites, as they had experienced exploitation and cruelty at their hands.

Jonah can be a confusing book – it certainly ends in a perplexing manner. But there are themes that feature strongly throughout: God's sovereignty, his mercy and compassion and the need for repentance. We might view God's mercy as being most apparent in the way he dealt with the Ninevites – and yet the patient way he dealt with Jonah is a powerful picture of his compassion too. While many view this story as far-fetched and fanciful (and some of the details do seem over the top), Jonah's story is actually pretty relatable and honest. Throughout this study, I will be asking: are we that different to Jonah?

No thanks, God!

But Jonah ran away from the Lord and headed for Tarshish. He went down to Joppa, where he found a ship… and sailed for Tarshish to flee from the Lord. (v. 3, NIV)

Right at the start God commissioned Jonah. This was nothing new – Jonah was God's prophet after all. So what *was* different? Rather than speaking to the Israelite king, God was asking him to speak a message condemning the wickedness of Nineveh. For Jonah, one would have been a known situation, where he received some level of respect, and the other a difficult journey to a hostile people. How do you respond when God asks you to move from your comfort zone? Do you embrace the change, however difficult, or try to ignore his request?

Jonah's response was to run in completely the opposite direction! If we are honest, are we that different? But was his response out of fear or anger? Jonah 4:2 sheds light on this – he had argued with God because he didn't like the sound of the message and knew that God was merciful. He didn't want the Ninevites to have a chance to repent. His mindset against them was at the heart of his disobedience. He felt he knew better than God.

Jonah soon learned that saying no to God has consequences! God was still in control of the situation, stirring up a storm once Jonah was aboard the boat. Jonah's actions affected all those onboard, just as our sin can hurt others. Interestingly, he was fast asleep below the deck. This reminds me of Jesus sleeping during a storm (see Mark 4:35–41). However, Jonah's sleep shows his conscience wasn't even pricked – he slept peacefully even though he was disobeying God. Our own conscience is not always a good measure of our holiness.

Finally, God used the crew's act of casting lots to show Jonah that he couldn't hide from him.

Lord, Jonah's story is a stark reminder to me that you are always in control. Help me to learn to say yes to you quickly, rather than running from your requests. Amen.

CLAIRE MUSTERS

Taking responsibility

'Pick me up and throw me into the sea,' he replied, 'and it will become calm. I know that it is my fault that this great storm has come upon you.' (v. 12, NIV)

The sailors already knew that Jonah was running away from God (v. 10), but once they had cast lots, they demanded to know more about who he was and what he was doing. He began by stating his racial identity: 'I am a Hebrew' – another clue that Jonah's attitude was one of racial superiority.

When Jonah explained that he worshipped 'the God of heaven, who made the sea and the dry land' (v. 9), it was abundantly clear to the ship's crew that they were in trouble. While they had been trying to call on their own gods, they recognised there was something more powerful about this one, who answered a runaway with a huge storm.

We can't run away from God and still expect to be under his protection. I learned this the hard way. After struggling with loneliness in the early years of our marriage when I hardly ever saw my husband, I left with another married man from my church. But right from the outset I pleaded with God not to take his presence from me. I had a heart for worship and had already been involved in church leadership. I was desperate for God not to leave me. (You can read more of my story in *Taking Off the Mask* and *Grace-filled Marriage*. Find out more at **clairemusters.com**.)

Like he did with Jonah, God patiently worked with me – even though there were painful consequences. Ultimately, I had to take responsibility for myself, which is what Jonah did here. He realised the storm was his fault (v. 12), so he began to think of others and threw himself on God's mercy by suggesting they throw him overboard. Don't miss the irony: he refused to go to the Ninevites because he viewed them as wicked foreigners, yet here he was willing to die for other foreigners who worshipped other gods.

Take some time to think about your own attitudes towards different people groups. Ask God to help you repent of any feelings of superiority. And today be conscious of taking responsibility for your own thoughts and actions.

CLAIRE MUSTERS

Worshipping a miracle-making God

Then they took Jonah and threw him overboard, and the raging sea grew calm. At this the men greatly feared the Lord. (vv. 15–16, NIV)

The actions of the sailors stand in great contrast to the superior attitude we have seen in Jonah. Their response to his directive to throw him overboard was to try everything else they could first, showing him more compassion than he had shown them. But when they realised there was nothing they could do, they cried out to God (v. 14) before throwing Jonah overboard (v. 15). When the storm immediately calmed, they responded by praying and vowing to serve God. We may have expected them to shout out terrified promises to God in the midst of the storm, but they actually did this once the sea was calm. They saw and recognised that God is able to do the miraculous.

The other great miracle here is the fish that God supplied to swallow Jonah. This is where the story seems far-fetched – but is that simply because it is so far outside our own experience? Do we question other miracles that we hear about? The beauty of this story is the way it foretells Jesus. Jonah was able to survive in the belly of the fish for three days, providing a picture of Jesus' death and resurrection. In fact, Jesus referred back to Jonah when speaking to religious leaders who were demanding a sign, saying: 'None will be given… except the sign of the prophet Jonah. For as Jonah was three days and three nights in the belly of a huge fish, so the Son of Man will be three days and three nights in the heart of the earth' (Matthew 12:39–40).

While those recounting the story of Jonah often say that being swallowed by the fish was the means by which Jonah was saved, it was, in fact, just the start of his journey towards understanding.

How do you respond when you hear news of a miracle? Ask God to keep your heart soft, so you recognise and rejoice when he is at work.

CLAIRE MUSTERS

A prayer of thanksgiving

But I, with shouts of grateful praise, will sacrifice to you. What I have vowed I will make good. I will say, 'Salvation comes from the Lord.' (v. 9, NIV)

Sometimes the most important lessons are learned in times of discomfort when God's mercy is at work behind the scenes. We can see this here: Jonah hadn't actually been fully rescued yet – unless God acted again, he would die inside the fish (so this wasn't a prayer of deliverance). But Jonah did appear, finally, to be beginning to learn something. He wasn't in the place of repentance yet, but he did recognise God at work and, by the end, vowed to do what God had told him to (v. 9). At that point, God commanded the fish to vomit him up. (Note the order: Jonah made his vow before he was saved from the fish.)

God was always in control. It was Jonah who had chosen to run and ended up in a downward spiral: going down to a boat, then the bottom of the boat, then the bottom of the sea. Thank God that, while he allows us to go through these painful journeys, he doesn't leave us. It was when I was back living with my parents that I realised my life had reached rock bottom. I thought I had lost everything: my marriage, my home, my church and possibly my work too. And yet God cared tenderly for me and ultimately delivered me and restored our marriage. It is helpful for me to look back when I'm in the midst of other storms and remember how he was at work.

There are other lessons from Jonah's prayer. He recognised that God did rescue him from inevitable drowning (vv. 5–6). He also commented that he cried out to God when his 'life was ebbing away' (v. 7). How often do we wait until we are desperate before turning to God in prayer? Let's be quick to speak to our heavenly Father.

It is a really helpful practice to look back over our days to see where God has been at work. Take time to do this towards the end of today, and then say your own prayer of thanksgiving to God.

CLAIRE MUSTERS

The God of second chances

Then the word of the Lord came to Jonah a second time: 'Go to the great city of Nineveh and proclaim to it the message I give you.'
(vv. 1–2, NIV)

At the start of this chapter, God reiterates his commission to Jonah. Pause and let that sink in. Jonah had wilfully disobeyed and taken action to try to ensure he wouldn't have to carry God's message to Nineveh. But God was giving him a second chance. Do you ever feel like you have messed up so much that God can't possibly give you another chance – and then amazingly discover that he does? That is what happened to my husband and me: we had been part of the leadership of a new church when our relationship imploded. Yes, I went back home, and yes, I faced the congregation I had hurt hugely, taking responsibility for my actions. It was one of the hardest things I have ever done. But then we wrestled with whether we were supposed to stay in that church (without even considering being part of the leadership again). On holiday and praying specifically about it, God stopped us in our tracks by saying: 'Didn't I call you there? Have I said anything different?' His words still held true, even though we thought we had disqualified ourselves through our sin and foolish mistakes. Today, my husband is the full-time pastor of that very same church. It always reminds me that God's plans and purposes cannot be thwarted.

Jonah finally travelled to Nineveh and spoke what God had told him to. If we do the same, we may be surprised at what happens and who responds – but, equally, we may never know the full fruit, as we could simply be part of someone's journey towards faith. Here, the wicked people of Nineveh took note and made an outward sign of their repentance through wearing sackcloth and fasting. God's warning to them had been clear: today we have many clear messages within his word, but how seriously do we take sin and repentance?

I have noticed a trend away from using the words 'sin' and 'repentance' in books and talks, for fear of putting people off – but God is absolutely serious about sin and the need to turn away from it. Are you?

CLAIRE MUSTERS

Angered by God's compassion

'Isn't this what I said, Lord, when I was still at home? That is what I tried to forestall by fleeing to Tarshish. I knew that you are a gracious and compassionate God, slow to anger and abounding in love, a God who relents from sending calamity.' (v. 2, NIV)

God had compassion on the Ninevites because of the actions they took, which showed their repentance. As James 1:22 says, we can't just pay lip service; we need to take action: 'Do not merely listen to the word, and so deceive yourselves. Do what it says.'

Jonah was certainly angry, but I wonder if he was also concerned about his own reputation: he had travelled far to pronounce judgement on the Ninevites, and it didn't happen. Did he feel that made him look foolish? When we are serving God, whose glory are we seeking? Jonah appeared to have forgotten his purpose, which originated in the words God spoke to Abraham: 'Through your offspring all nations on earth will be blessed' (Genesis 22:18). God's message was to go out into all the world.

Jonah was all bent out of shape by God showing mercy, but God wasn't going against his word by turning away his wrath – in Jeremiah 18:7–8 it says: 'If at any time I announce that a nation or kingdom is to be uprooted, torn down and destroyed, and if that nation I warned repents of its evil, then I will relent and not inflict on it the disaster I had planned.'

Jonah quickly went from being happy he had been saved to angry when God saved those he didn't like. He didn't want the Ninevites forgiven; he wanted them destroyed. Are there times when we hold a similar view? Have we forgotten that we don't deserve God's forgiveness either?

Jonah was rather overdramatic, but at least he was finally honest. What do we do if we don't understand what God is up to – or we don't agree? It is important to be honest before him, but we must also be open to him challenging us, as he did Jonah.

Are there times you can bring to mind when you were angered by the way God dealt with others, feeling it wasn't fair? What did you do? Ask God to align your heart afresh with his today.

CLAIRE MUSTERS

God's final word

But the Lord said, 'You have been concerned about this plant, though you did not tend it or make it grow. It sprang up overnight and died overnight. And should I not have concern for the great city of Nineveh?' (vv. 10–11, NIV)

Jonah decided to sulk outside the city, where God provided for his discomfort in the form of a vine. Then God took the comfort away to show Jonah how petty and self-absorbed he could be. Jonah was angrier about the withering of a vine than what could have happened to Nineveh. How often do we complain to God at things we think are unjust when he is actually asking us to be more aware of his perspective?

We can be so much more sensitive to our own needs than to the spiritual needs of those around us. Jonah had to learn, as do we, not to be focused on what God can do for us, but to reach out to the world of the broken, forgotten and, yes, even wicked. I am reminded of a prayer meeting I was in recently, where we were praying for our borough and town, particularly focusing on the rise in knife crime. We prayed for protection for those going about their daily business, but we were also led to pray for those who were in the gangs, wielding the knives. Some even prayed that we would be those that do not flee from them scared but walk across to engage and share God's love with them. We need to be sensible and safe, but I found those prayers really challenging. Do I just focus my prayers on the people I feel deserve God's help?

As we finish our reflections, notice that God delivered all those who called on him in this book – the sailors, Jonah and the Ninevites. Their race and background did not matter. Prayer works, and it changes us. But who had the final word? God. We are left hanging, as we don't know how Jonah responded to God's challenging questions. But how will you?

Soberly reflect on whether you care more for your comfort than for reaching those God is sending you to. Ask him to make you aware of any prejudices you might have and repent of those.

CLAIRE MUSTERS

Finding God in unexpected places

Catherine Butcher writes:

Throughout the Bible there are people who met with God in the least likely places. God seems to delight in unexpected encounters. Over the next two weeks we will be looking at Old and New Testament characters who met with God. Some, like Moses, Mary Magdalene and Zacchaeus, are well-known names. Others are anonymous: a boy with a picnic lunch, a child on Jesus' knee, a man suffering from leprosy and two unnamed women – one drawing water at a well, the other caught in adultery.

For each of the characters, I have found a contemporary story with a similar theme to show that God doesn't change. Then I've aimed to apply the lessons of scripture to our own circumstances today.

The common thread seems to be that God is full of surprises. He appears to delight in surprising us with his strength when we admit our weakness and ask for his help. He seeks out the weakest and most insignificant people and elevates them to achieve his purposes, enabled by his power at work through them. He chooses the outcasts and untouchables, reaching out with love and acceptance.

The apostle Paul explained it this way:

I was given a physical condition which has been a thorn in my flesh, a messenger from Satan to hurt and bother me and prick my pride. Three different times I begged God to make me well again. Each time he said, 'No. But I am with you; that is all you need. My power shows up best in weak people'… When I am weak, then I am strong – the less I have, the more I depend on him.
2 Corinthians 12:7–10, TLB

I hope that through these next 14 days you will become more alert to hearing God's voice; more in tune with his priorities and more readily able to move out of your comfort zone to respond to God's call.

God wants us to know his intimate love; to enjoy the beauty of our wonderful world and to join him on an amazing adventure that goes on into eternity. That may mean finding him in unexpected places and introducing him to others, those the world might see as outcasts and untouchables.

Trusting God's promises

The Lord had said to Abram, 'Go from your country, your people and your father's household to the land I will show you.' (v. 1, NIV)

When I was in my teens my dad was made redundant. He was out of work for six months before he found a job. We lived in Edinburgh at the time. All our family and friends lived there, but the new job was in south London. Dad and Mum were praying about whether to take the job and move the family 400 miles to what seemed like a new country, when this verse came up in Dad's daily Bible reading. He phoned Scripture Union in London to ask what church they would recommend for a young family in the south London area, then he started house-hunting around that church in Purley, Surrey.

The first time he attended a service at the church, this verse was the theme of the sermon. Then the house he visited belonged to a couple from that church – their children had Sunday school work on their bedroom walls. It was a remarkable set of signs that confirmed to Dad that God was calling us to move south.

Today's Bible story starts with Abram setting out with his father and his extended family to go to Canaan. But when they came to Harran, they settled. God's unexpected challenge then came to Abram, calling him out of his comfort zone to go to the promised land of Canaan. Abram had to leave his old life and to trust in God's plan for his future.

God's call to Abram reminds us of our own call to obey God and follow his plans. It challenges us to leave behind our old lives and to trust in God's promises, even when they seem impossible or uncertain. It also encourages us to prioritise the things we value most and to trust in God's faithfulness.

Think about what God has called you to do and to be. Have you settled or are you still seeking to follow God's guidance? Recommit your life to him today.

CATHERINE BUTCHER

Meeting God in dreams

'All peoples on earth will be blessed through you and your offspring.
I am with you and will watch over you wherever you go.'
(vv. 14–15, NIV)

Abdul met Jesus in a dream while awaiting deportation from Heathrow's Immigration Removal Centre. There he had been befriended by a Nigerian Christian detainee who introduced him to the Bible. After reading it one night, Abdul had a dream.

Telling his story for the Lent book *40 Stories of Hope* (CWR, 2017), Abdul said: 'It was 4.30 am. All the world was very dark, but then a person appeared, shining like light. I couldn't look at his face. I said, "Who are you?" He said, "I am Jesus, the Messiah." I said, "Who are all these other people?" He said, "These are all the people who love me." And then I woke up. I couldn't sleep. I stood and thought about it, and then I came to the chapel. I think that Jesus is my friend to tell me about himself like that.'

Abdul started reading a Bible in his native language. 'The Bible gives me everything I need really,' he says. 'When I read it, I become relaxed and I forget that I'm in the detention centre. It makes me very happy.'

Abdul's and Jacob's encounters with God in dreams remind us that God can meet us in unexpected ways and places. Jacob, Abraham's grandson, was on a journey to his uncle Laban's house when he stopped to rest for the night. Jacob was always scheming and plotting to get what he wanted. He had tricked his brother Esau out of his birthright. But God didn't reprimand him. Instead, God revealed himself and gave Jacob this amazing promise.

Let's be encouraged by this story to trust that God is with us in the ordinary moments of our lives, and let's be open to the ways that God might choose to communicate with us.

Father God, thank you that you are at work in our world, revealing yourself to people like Abdul as well as to Jacob and many other Bible characters long ago. Help me to be aware of you in every situation. Amen.

CATHERINE BUTCHER

Stopped in his tracks

Moses said to God, 'Who am I that I should go to Pharaoh and bring the Israelites out of Egypt?' (v. 11, NIV)

We were on holiday in Yorkshire when I received an unexpected phone call. Would I be available to edit the Mothers' Union's national magazine, and could I start straight away to fill in a gap left by the editor's long-term sickness? Mothers' Union had found a tiny mention of my work in the UK Christian Handbook that led to the call.

I had taken a three-month sabbatical, stopping all my work as a journalist and editor, wanting to find fresh direction from God, so I was available to start the next week. I was amazed to find that much of my previous experience dovetailed with the magazine's needs.

Moses was looking after his father-in-law's flock when he saw the burning bush. He was curious and, as he approached it, God spoke to him. The encounter transformed Moses' life and set him on a new path to become a great leader who would deliver the Israelites from slavery in Egypt. Although he felt inadequate (v. 11), he was in fact uniquely qualified for the role. He had been brought up as the adopted son of Pharaoh's daughter, so had an extraordinary insight into Egyptian life.

Often, God speaks to us in unexpected ways, and we may not even realise that it is him until we stop our normal routine to listen and pay attention. God might use ordinary or extraordinary things to get our attention. It is up to us to have open hearts and minds to receive what he has to say to us.

Moses had left Egypt as a murderer on the run. He must have assumed that he would never return, but God had other plans. Like Moses, when we encounter God in unexpected ways, we can trust that he has equipped us for the task he has for us.

Moses, John the Baptist, Jesus… maybe you? God has a habit of calling people out of a desert experience to work for him. What is God saying to you today?

CATHERINE BUTCHER

The weakest and the least

'Pardon me, my lord,' Gideon replied, 'but how can I save Israel? My clan is the weakest in Manasseh, and I am the least in my family.' (v. 15, NIV)

TV presenter James Lusted is just 3ft 7in. He was born with diastrophic dysplasia, a rare disorder that causes dwarfism. In an interview with Jen Johnson for *Hope for All* magazine, he recalled one day when he was just 15 years old, he came home after a day facing school bullies and went straight to his room to hide under his duvet. His mum's words made all the difference: 'James, you are made in the image of Christ. It doesn't matter who you are, or the way you are – you can do everything, just in a different way – and you can use your voice to ask people to help you. God has a plan and a purpose for you, and he wants you to see life and live it to the full.'

James says, 'It was like a switch in my heart just flicked on. From that day onwards, I went into school and started to stand up for myself. Yes, I am different, but that's okay.'*

God found Gideon threshing grain in a winepress. He was afraid and saw himself as the weakest and the least in his family. God saw him differently. He described Gideon as 'a mighty warrior' (v. 12) who was to save Israel.

God can use anyone for his purposes. Gideon was not a great warrior or a charismatic leader. He was an ordinary man from an ordinary family. But God saw something in him that others did not and chose him to be a powerful instrument in his hands. God promised to be with Gideon and to give him victory, and he did just that.

Gideon's encounter teaches us to trust in God, to obey his commands and to believe in his power to accomplish great things through us, even when we feel weak or inadequate.

* You can read the whole article at **hopeforall.org.uk/read/passion-for-life-2**.

Give to God the challenges you are facing this week and pray, 'Heavenly Father, help me to see myself as you see me and to trust you in all circumstances. Amen.'

CATHERINE BUTCHER

God speaks

The Lord called, 'Samuel!' And Samuel got up and went to Eli and said, 'Here I am; you called me.' (v. 8, NIV)

Sarah longed to be married. Telling me her story, she said she had been befriended by a young man in her church and was wondering if he might be 'the one'. As they spent time together, she found herself growing closer to him. Then one night she woke up suddenly. All feelings for the young man had disappeared. She felt as if God was warning her not to take the relationship any further. Sometime later she discovered that the man was already married and had a child but was separated from his wife and had moved from one church to another befriending young, unmarried women. Sarah felt that her unexpected encounter with God that night had saved her lots of pain and anguish.

As a young boy, Samuel heard God calling him by name, but he didn't recognise God's voice. He thought it was his mentor, Eli. But Eli realised that it was God speaking. Through this encounter, God revealed his plan for Samuel's life as a prophet and leader.

God can speak to us in unexpected ways: Samuel was not expecting to hear from God, but God chose to speak to him. God might choose to speak to us through a variety of means: through other people, circumstances, dreams or in quiet moments of prayer and reflection. It's important to keep our minds and hearts open to these unexpected encounters with God.

When Samuel realised that it was God speaking to him, he responded with obedience and humility. In the same way, we need to be attentive to God's voice so we can respond willingly to do what he asks of us, even if it means setting aside our own desires and plans to follow God's lead.

Samuel's encounter with God came while he was under Eli's guidance. Ask God to give you a mentor or spiritual guides to help you discern God's voice and test what you believe he is saying to you.

CATHERINE BUTCHER

Changed forever

'Do not be afraid of what they say or be terrified by them, though they are a rebellious people. You must speak my words to them, whether they listen or fail to listen.' (2:6–7, NIV)

In 1972, Mary Kay was arrested, convicted and sentenced to 21 years in an Alabama prison after a string of bank robberies. Flipping through a Bible one evening, she read Ezekiel 36:26: 'I will give you a new heart and put a new spirit in you.'

In her cell that night she prayed, 'Okay, if you will do that for me, I will give the rest of my life back to you.'

Mary Kay became a Christian and founded Angel Tree, a Prison Fellowship programme designed to share God's love by helping to meet the physical, emotional and spiritual needs of the families of prisoners. She is one of many people through the ages whose life has been changed because she responded to God as a result of hearing about him through Ezekiel.

Ezekiel's encounter with God changed him forever. His vision of God was not what he expected. God appeared to him as a fiery chariot with four living creatures, each with four faces. After this startling vision, God called Ezekiel to be a faithful witness to the people of Israel, even though they were rebellious and disobedient, and it was difficult for him. When God called Ezekiel to be a prophet, he also gave him the strength and courage to fulfil this calling. God made him resilient (3:9) and Ezekiel sensed 'the strong hand of the Lord on me' (3:14).

Jesus has called each of us to be his witnesses. Our contemporaries might not be interested in our faith, but our calling is to be faithful to Jesus – to focus on him and to trust that he is at work, even if we don't immediately see the outcome we hope for.

Take time today to pray for the people you see week by week, who don't yet know Jesus as Saviour. Ask God to use you to witness to his love.

CATHERINE BUTCHER

Lessons from the life-giver

After three days they found him in the temple courts, sitting among the teachers, listening to them and asking them questions. Everyone who heard him was amazed at his understanding and his answers. (vv. 46–47, NIV)

I once interviewed astrophysicist David Wilkinson about the evidence base for his faith. Was it compatible with his scientific background? He said:

I see a number of significant pointers in the universe, such as the beauty and intelligibility of the laws of physics, the extraordinary balances in law and circumstance which make possible carbon-based life, and the sense of awe that we feel when we see the diversity and simplicity of the universe. However, the main evidence does not come from science. It comes from the evidence of the life, death and resurrection of Jesus of Nazareth, which for me can only be explained by the Christian belief that here in Jesus was God himself walking in the space history of the universe. At the heart of my Christian faith is the conviction and the experience that God has revealed himself supremely in the life, death and resurrection of Jesus of Nazareth – and I encounter him in the Bible and in my day-to-day experience.
HOPE magazine, December 2016

For someone like David Wilkinson, Jesus satisfied his intellectual curiosity; but it is his daily encounter with Jesus through scripture and experience that compels him to follow Jesus.

The teachers in the temple courts didn't expect a young boy to be able to discuss anything with them. They were surprised by their encounter with the creator of the universe in the human form of a boy. But if their question-and-answer session only led to an intellectual response, they were missing out. Like David Wilkinson, we each need to respond to Jesus' life, death and resurrection. He is the life-giver. He wants to give us his new life and to spend it with him as he walks and talks with us throughout life's journey.

Ask God to show you more of his glory in the wonders of the created world. Take time to notice the beauty of nature around you and be thankful.

CATHERINE BUTCHER

Loved into life

He took a little child whom he placed among them. Taking the child in his arms, he said to them, 'Whoever welcomes one of these little children in my name welcomes me.' (vv. 36–37, NIV)

Raj was just 16 when she tried to kill herself. 'I started taking these tablets. I just wanted to be dead.' When her dad found out, he said, 'It's a shame it didn't work.'

Raj was interviewed as part of the 'Talking Jesus' series produced by Hope Together. One night as she was crying, she heard a voice saying, 'Raj, stop crying.'

'I knew it was God,' she said. 'I felt love. I didn't really know what love was as I'd never experienced it, but I recognised it was love.'

That night, as she felt God's love for the first time, she found herself forgiving her family for the way she had been treated. Later, thinking about Jesus' death and resurrection, she says, 'It just clicked, what Jesus has done for me. He saved me! I wanted to be dead, and he gave me life.'

Jesus reached out to Raj, just as he reached out to the child in today's Bible reading. Imagine what it was like for that child to be held in Jesus' arms, to be the example of greatness that Jesus chose when the disciples were busy arguing among themselves about who was the greatest. Jesus chose the child, showing them that the least among them was the most important.

It's as if the disciples wanted to change the subject when they asked Jesus about someone driving out demons in his name. But Jesus is not deflected. He answers their questions and returns to focus on the child, showing how precious children are to him.

Do you know how much you are loved by God? Does your church welcome and prioritise children so they can know God's love from an early age?

List the children in your church or those known to you among your family and friends. Pray for each one by name, asking God to show them how much they are loved by him.

CATHERINE BUTCHER

An unexpected touch

'Lord, if you are willing, you can make me clean.' Jesus reached out his hand and touched the man. 'I am willing,' he said. 'Be clean!' (vv. 12–13, NIV)

Joanne O'Connor is the CEO of Junction 42, a Christian prison charity. She is always listening to God and looking for ways to make a difference, building relationships and pointing people to Jesus. Chatting to some of the men she met in prison, she discovered that they felt their hair was an important part of their identity, but the prison barber simply shaved everyone's head in the same way.

Joanne thought, 'What would it be like for someone to come in and teach them how to braid each other's hair?' So Junction 42 set about overcoming the considerable obstacles to set up the first 'Wing Barbers'. As a result, Joanne found that the atmosphere in the prison changed. As the men touched each other and trusted each other, the aggression was reduced.

For the man with leprosy, Jesus' touch made all the difference. He had heard that Jesus healed people, so he came to beg Jesus to cure him. He would have been shunned by everyone, since the first signs of leprosy marked him out as unclean. He might have heard that Jesus had healed others at a distance, so Jesus' touch must have come as a surprise. The man was no longer untouchable. Jesus healed him physically, but also healed his emotions.

As you read through the gospels, notice how Jesus treats everyone as an individual. Each healing is different. There is no formula. Sometimes he uses words, sometimes touch; he even used mud made with his own spit to heal a blind man (John 9:6)! Are you listening to God so he can use you to meet the needs of others? Are you ready to be surprised by what he asks you to do?

Pray today for those you meet this week, asking God to show you how to reach out to them in ways that bring them closer to Jesus.

CATHERINE BUTCHER

Practical repentance

Zacchaeus stood up and said to the Lord, 'Look, Lord! Here and now I give half of my possessions to the poor, and if I have cheated anybody out of anything, I will pay back four times the amount.' (v. 8, NIV)

Gary Grant and his wife started a toy business in 1981 called The Entertainer. He became a Christian ten years later and says, 'That changed everything.'

He admits he had a lot to learn. When a local Christian accountant challenged him about his finances, Gary told Roy Crowne of the ministry Gospel Entrepreneurs: 'I was sort of wheeling and dealing. That was the old Gary, but with the new Gary, one of the areas of major change was the area of honesty. Maybe I wasn't paying as much tax back in the early eighties or the mid-eighties that I could have done. So I had to look at every aspect of the business and make sure that I was really prepared to be open for scrutiny.'

Also, when his wife brought up the subject of tithing, Gary didn't know what she meant. But now The Entertainer gives 10% of its net annual profit to charity each year. It is also an active member of the Pennies scheme, which enables customers to donate a few pence to charity when paying by card.

Becoming a follower of Jesus changed Gary's attitude to money, just as Zacchaeus' encounter with Jesus changed him. Many people saw Zacchaeus as a traitor because of his job as a tax collector. Although he had money and status and was marginalised by his community, Jesus showed him compassion and love. Zacchaeus immediately became radical about generosity. Jesus hadn't told him to give anything away, but being in Jesus' presence prompted Zacchaeus to give half of his possessions to the poor. This practical act of repentance led to his salvation.

Have you allowed Jesus to challenge your finances? Are you giving regularly and, if your circumstances allow it, using Gift Aid to maximise the impact of your gift?

Meditate on this verse: 'Each of you should give what you have decided in your heart to give, not reluctantly or under compulsion, for God loves a cheerful giver' (2 Corinthians 9:7).

CATHERINE BUTCHER

An expert's valuation

Many of the Samaritans from that town believed in him because of the woman's testimony, 'He told me everything I've ever done'… They said to the woman, 'We no longer believe just because of what you said; now we have heard for ourselves, and we know that this man really is the Saviour of the world.' (v. 39 and v. 42, NIV)

Vivien's sister died leaving some jewellery, and Vivien had decided to sell it at auction. The auction house told her that one of the rings was worthless, unmarked metal with paste gems. But the expert who put the jewellery up for sale listed the ring as 15 carat gold with white sapphires. It took the expert to know its true worth.

This Samaritan woman's encounter with Jesus in today's reading is now known worldwide. She came to draw water from the well at midday when no one else was around. Perhaps she felt worthless and ashamed because of her past life. By approaching her and asking her for a drink, Jesus was breaking many cultural taboos.

Jews and Samaritans had a longstanding feud, so Jews avoided Samaria, walking round it rather than travelling through it. It was considered taboo for a Jewish man to talk to a Samaritan woman, particularly one-to-one with a woman who was not a relative. What Jesus did was scandalous.

In Jesus' time, it was not common for a rabbi to teach a woman, and even less so about spiritual matters. However, Jesus teaches the Samaritan woman about worship and salvation and reveals his identity as the Messiah. Even though Jews considered Samaritans to be unclean, Jesus was willing to accept a drink from her cup. Jesus was making himself vulnerable asking for a drink, and that in itself showed her she wasn't worthless. She might have seen herself as an outcast, but Jesus saw her true worth as a woman who was to introduce her whole town to the Saviour of the world.

Like the woman at the well, you might feel worthless, but Jesus is the expert who knows your true worth. He loves you enough to give his life for you.

'Give me this water so that I won't get thirsty' (v. 15). Echo this prayer as you think about the areas of your life where you need Jesus to meet your needs.

CATHERINE BUTCHER

God's provision

'There's a youngster here with five barley loaves and a couple of fish!
But what good is that with all this mob?' (vv. 8–9, TLB)

In her book *The Cox's Book of Modern Saints and Martyrs*, Baroness Caroline
Cox tells the story of Sister Maria Lourdes, who sheltered 15,000 people in
the forest around her house in East Timor, when fighting in the region was
at its worst.

'We didn't have enough food for 15 people, never mind 15,000,' she said.
'But each day I got up, I prayed, and then I started cooking rice – and the
barrel of rice never ran out for three weeks. The day it ran out was the day
the international peacekeepers came.'

Sister Maria felt totally inadequate, but God used her to provide food
for those frightened, hungry people, just as he provided miraculously for
5,000 men and their families 2,000 years ago using a boy's picnic lunch.
Imagine the boy's surprise when the disciples requisitioned his small meal
and started sharing it with such a large crowd. I wonder how his encounter
with Jesus changed him. Did he realise that God 'is able to do immeasur-
ably more than all we ask or imagine' (Ephesians 3:2, NIV).

In the story, Philip was the realist. He calculated that, humanly speaking, it would be impossible to feed the people with what they had. Andrew
had a glimmer of faith, but still doubted that the loaves and fish could
make a difference. But the boy gave what he had, and God did the rest. All
were amazed at the miracle.

You may well feel inadequate and ill-equipped. But are you willing to
trust God with what little you have, to allow him to work his miracles in
your life? God seems to delight in surprising us with his strength, when we
admit our weakness and ask for his help.

---

*Are there areas of your life where you need to ask God for forgiveness for your
self-reliance and lack of trust? Give your finances, relationships and responsibilities to him, thanking him and asking him to surprise you.*

CATHERINE BUTCHER

No condemnation

'Woman, where are they? Has no one condemned you?' 'No one, sir,' she said. 'Then neither do I condemn you,' Jesus declared. 'Go now and leave your life of sin.' (vv. 10–11, NIV)

'I lacked confidence, struggled at school and was left with low self-esteem,' John (not his real name) told me. He became a Christian at a Spring Harvest event. Tragically he was befriended by a paedophile when he was twelve years old, then groomed and sexually abused by him until he was 17, when he managed to walk away. It was ten years before he went to the police and eventually saw the perpetrator go to prison for a substantial period of time.

Now John works in prisons as a chaplain and says, 'What a strange turnaround in life when God uses the abused to minister to the abuser! God is a master at this stuff. He takes the unconfident, bruised and beaten, the abused and hopeless, neglected and manipulated child on a journey, led by his hand through a redemptive circle towards wholeness. Then he uses that child of his, years later, to bring good news to the poor, to bring true freedom to the prisoner, to bring healing to the damaged, to bring freedom to the oppressed in Jesus' name.' John was surprised at how God has used him.

What a surprise for this woman who was brought before Jesus. She was expecting to be stoned. Instead, Jesus used her to teach the teachers of the law and the Pharisees a lesson. Rather than condemning her, Jesus offers her grace and an opportunity to start afresh. We don't know how her story turned out – she isn't mentioned in the other gospels – and we don't know if her life was turned around by her encounter with Jesus.

As you look back on your life, are there areas where you have been healed and set free. How is God using you now to bring healing and freedom to others?

Jesus told Nicodemus: 'God did not send his Son into the world to condemn the world, but to save the world through him' (John 3:17). Spend some time thanking God for what he has done in your life.

CATHERINE BUTCHER

Outcasts welcome

Thinking he was the gardener, she said, 'Sir, if you have carried him away, tell me where you have put him, and I will get him.' Jesus said to her, 'Mary.' (vv. 15–16, NIV)

Trudy Makepeace grew up living as though she had 'victim' written on her forehead, she says. In her book *Abused, Addicted, Free* (Malcolm Down Publishing, 2021), she describes her childhood: starved of love; abused physically, emotionally and sexually; bullied and tormented at both home and school. That led to an 18-year battle with drug addiction, living and working on the streets and spending time in prison.

'After 33 failed attempts to get clean, I had finally lost all hope that I could fix me, that I could change,' she says. That's when she became open to Jesus' love.

She remembers, 'I encountered the overwhelming love and presence of God… I fully surrendered my life to Jesus and handed him all my brokenness. In that moment, he took the weight of my sin and shame.'

Now, years later, she works as an outreach and evangelism minister for a church in Bristol. Her life has been transformed and God has made her a true champion of the broken, destitute and marginalised people in the city where she was once an addict.

When Jesus first met Mary Magdalene, he delivered her from seven demons (Luke 8:2). She would have been an outcast, but her life was transformed and she joined the twelve disciples as one of the women supporting them out of their own means.

In today's reading, Mary was among the first witnesses to Jesus' resurrection. When he called her by name, she recognised him. Mary Magdalene then went to the disciples with the news: 'I have seen the Lord!' (v. 18).

Her unexpected encounter with Jesus in the garden was world changing. He had touched her personal life, setting her free. Now he was using her to tell her world about the resurrection life of Jesus and that message has continued to spread throughout history.

Thank God for his transforming love at work in your life. Continue to pray for those you know who are yet to experience the freedom Jesus brings.

CATHERINE BUTCHER

BRF Ministries

Inspiring people of all ages to grow in Christian faith

BRF Ministries is the
home of Anna Chaplaincy,
Living Faith, Messy Church
and Parenting for Faith

As a charity, our work would not be possible without
fundraising and gifts in wills.
To find out more and to donate,
visit brf.org.uk/give or call +44 (0)1235 462305

Registered with
FUNDRAISING
REGULATOR

To order

Online: **brfonline.org.uk**
Telephone: **+44 (0)1865 319700**
Mon–Fri 9.30–17.00

Delivery times within the UK are normally 15 working days. Prices are correct at the time of going to press but may change without prior notice.

Title	Price	Qty	Total
Day by Day with God (May–Aug 2024) – single copy	£4.99		
Day by Day with God (Sep–Dec 2024) – single copy	£4.99		

POSTAGE AND PACKING CHARGES			
Order value	UK	Europe	Rest of world
Under £7.00	£2.00	Available on request	Available on request
£7.00–£29.99	£3.00		
£30.00 and over	FREE		

Total value of books	
Donation	
Postage and packing	
Total for this order	

Please complete in BLOCK CAPITALS

Title .... First name/initials .... Surname ....

Address ....

.... Postcode ....

Acc. No. .... Telephone ....

Email ....

Method of payment

❑ Cheque (made payable to BRF) ❑ MasterCard / Visa

Card no. ☐☐☐☐ ☐☐☐☐ ☐☐☐☐ ☐☐☐☐

Expires end ☐M☐M ☐Y☐Y Security code ☐☐☐   Last 3 digits on the reverse of the card

We will use your personal data to process this order.
From time to time we may send you information about the work of BRF Ministries. Please contact us if you wish to discuss your mailing preferences. Our privacy possible is available at **brf.org.uk/privacy**.

Please return this form to:
BRF Ministries, 15 The Chambers, Vineyard, Abingdon OX14 3FE | **enquiries@brf.org.uk**
For terms and cancellation information, please visit **brfonline.org.uk/terms**.

Each issue of *Day by Day with God* is available from Christian bookshops everywhere. Copies may also be available through your church book agent or from the person who distributes Bible reading notes in your church.

Alternatively, you may obtain *Day by Day with God* on subscription direct from the publisher. There are two kinds of subscription:

Individual subscription
covering 3 issues for 4 copies or less, payable in advance
(including postage & packing).

To order, please complete the details on page 144 and return with the appropriate payment to: BRF Ministries, 15 The Chambers, Vineyard, Abingdon OX14 3FE

You can also use the form on page 144 to order a gift subscription for a friend.

Group subscription
covering 3 issues for 5 copies or more, sent to one UK address (post free).

Please note that the annual billing period for group subscriptions runs from 1 May to 30 April.

To order, please complete the details on page 143 and return with the appropriate payment to: BRF Ministries, 15 The Chambers, Vineyard, Abingdon OX14 3FE

You will receive an invoice with the first issue of notes.

> All our Bible reading notes can be ordered online by visiting
> **brfonline.org.uk/collections/subscriptions**

All subscription enquiries should be directed to:
BRF Ministries, 15 The Chambers, Vineyard, Abingdon OX14 3FE
+44 (0)1865 319700 | enquiries@brf.org.uk

DBDWG0224

DAY BY DAY WITH GOD GROUP SUBSCRIPTION FORM

> All our Bible reading notes can be ordered online by visiting
> **brfonline.org.uk/collections/subscriptions**

The group subscription rate for *Day by Day with God* will be £14.97 per person until April 2025.

☐ I would like to take out a group subscription for _____ (quantity) copies.

☐ Please start my order with the September 2024 / January 2025 / May 2025* issue. I would like to pay annually/receive an invoice* with each edition of the notes. (*delete as appropriate)

Please do not send any money with your order. Send your order to BRF and we will send you an invoice.

Name and address of the person organising the group subscription:

Title _____ First name/initials _____ Surname _____

Address_____

_____ Postcode _____

Telephone _____ Email _____

Church_____

Name and address of the person paying the invoice if the invoice needs to be sent directly to them:

Title _____ First name/initials _____ Surname _____

Address_____

_____ Postcode _____

Telephone _____ Email _____

We will use your personal data to process this order. From time to time we may send you information about the work of BRF Ministries. Please contact us if you wish to discuss your mailing preferences. Our privacy policy is available at **brf.org.uk/privacy.**

Please return this form to:
BRF Ministries, 15 The Chambers, Vineyard, Abingdon OX14 3FE |
enquiries@brf.org.uk

For terms and cancellation information, please visit **brfonline.org.uk/terms.**

Bible Reading Fellowship is a charity (233280) and company limited by guarantee (301324), registered in England and Wales

To order online, please visit **brfonline.org.uk/collections/subscriptions**

☐ I would like to give a gift subscription (please provide both names and addresses)

☐ I would like to take out a subscription myself (complete your name and address details only once)

Title _____ First name/initials _____ Surname _____

Address _____

_____ Postcode _____

Telephone _____ Email _____

Gift subscription name _____

Gift subscription address _____

_____ Postcode _____

Gift subscription (20 words max. or include your own gift card):

_____

_____

Please send *Day by Day with God* beginning with the September 2024 / January 2025 / May 2025 issue (*delete as appropriate*):

(*please tick box*)	UK	Europe	Rest of world
1-year subscription	☐ £19.50	☐ £26.85	☐ £30.75
2-year subscription	☐ £38.40	N/A	N/A

Optional donation to support the work of BRF Ministries £ _____

Total enclosed £ _____ (cheques should be made payable to 'BRF')

Please charge my MasterCard / Visa with £ _____

Card no. ☐☐☐☐ ☐☐☐☐ ☐☐☐☐ ☐☐☐☐

Expires end ☐☐ M M ☐☐ Y Y   Security code ☐☐☐   Last 3 digits on the reverse of the card

We will use your personal data to process this order. From time to time we may send you information about the work of BRF Ministries. Please contact us if you wish to discuss your mailing preferences. Our privacy policy is available at **brf.org.uk/privacy.**

Please return this form to:
BRF Ministries, 15 The Chambers, Vineyard, Abingdon OX14 3FE |
enquiries@brf.org.uk

For terms and cancellation information, please visit **brfonline.org.uk/terms.**

Bible Reading Fellowship is a charity (233280) and company limited by guarantee (301324), registered in England and Wales

DBDWG0224